ROCK BOTTOM
Inspired by God

MICHAEL TETER

WESTBOW
PRESS
A DIVISION OF THOMAS NELSON

WestBow Press books may be ordered through booksellers or by contacting:

WestBow Press
A Division of Thomas Nelson
1663 Liberty Drive
Bloomington, IN 47403
www.westbowpress.com
1-(866) 928-1240

Because of the dynamic nature of the Internet, any web addresses or links contained in this book may have changed since publication and may no longer be valid. The views expressed in this work are solely those of the author and do not necessarily reflect the views of the publisher, and the publisher hereby disclaims any responsibility for them.

Any people depicted in stock imagery provided by Thinkstock are models, and such images are being used for illustrative purposes only.

Certain stock imagery © Thinkstock.

ISBN: 978-1-4497-8112-5 (sc)

Library of Congress Control Number: 2013900002

Scripture quotations taken from the Holy Bible, New Living Translation, copyright 1996, 2004. Used by permission of Tyndale House Publishers, Inc., Wheaton, Illinois 60189. All rights reserved.

Printed in the United States of America

WestBow Press rev. date: 06/04/2013

BIOGRAPHY

He was born in a small town, Garnett, KS. His father was an alcoholic and his mother a truly strong woman. He is the youngest of five children. His dad told him he would always be a no body. He began getting in trouble with the law at age nine. Desperately seeking the love his heart longed for he continued to act oHe was arrested over twenty times, leading to many years in prison. During his last prison sentence his father was diagnosed with Lou Gerig's Disease. His dad was taken to Lansing Maximum State Prison to see his son. He saw his father in a wheel chair and was awe struck. The only thing his father was able to whisper to him is I hope your'e saved some day kid. He went back to his cell and said God if you are real show me. That's when it all began, and this is his story. He's been out of prison since December 03, 2009, currently resides in Richmond, Kansas, and works as a metal fabricator in Ottawa, Kansas. He is the appointed leader of S.P.I.R.I.T Ministries, manages a website, wrote a book, inspirational speaker of God, has his own singing ministry called the UNSCENE band, has went back into Lansing Prison and shared Jesus Christ with his inmate friends, and continues to seek God ceaselessly. He just wants to share the joy God has given him that another may experience it.

DEDICATION

I would like to dedicate this book to God, for I give God all glory, honor, and praise. A part from him I could accomplish nothing. I also dedicate this book to my dad who God used to speak those words to me in my darkest hour. Thank you dad, I love you and I miss you. Thank you God for all things. May you rest in peace pops, I will see you again one day. That will be a celebration. I can do all things through Christ who gives me the strength I need. Philippians 4:13 NLT.

ROCK BOTTOM

Inspired by God

I'm going to attempt to take you to a place many people have never been, nor thought about. As I tell you this story, I feel that it is imperative that you know that I, as a man give all glory to God for this opportunity. I would not be doing this if it weren't for my Lord and Savior Jesus Christ. I have humbled myself, so I just listen after praying for direction. I pray that these words bring new meaning and inspiration to the person that is reading it. May the good Lord continue to bless you beyond your imagination. I pray in the name of Jesus Christ, Amen.

As a young boy I struggled with life just like any other kid. I am the youngest of five children, one brother and three beautiful sisters. My father was a good man who raised me the best of his ability. He was a struggling alcoholic, God bless his soul, and my mother is a truly strong woman. They had their good times and their bad times just like any other relationship. However, we all suffered greatly when my pops would come home drunk in the wee hours of the morning and wake us all up and verbally abuse us to no end. My mom cried a lot, but she went on like nothing ever happened. I didn't know any better, I thought it was normal for the majority of my life.

I kept this to myself for many, many years. I just wanted to be released from the abuse and I often wondered if all of the other kids were going through the same things we were. It just didn't seem fair to me. It was overwhelming and I just didn't understand why it continued to happen. Years later I came to the understanding that we learn from our peers; parents, teachers, and close friends of our family. I said to myself, doesn't it make sense that the way I was raised reflects the way my parents were raised as well. It certainly does. I know that they didn't have the greatest childhood and essentially when they married and had children they did the best with what they were given. This is how I began to understand that life is what we make it. You can set around and feel sorry for yourself or you can take charge of it and go get it. Only you can do it, no one is going to do it for you and that is just the simple truth. The world owes us absolutely nothing.

I didn't know it at the time but the dysfunctional behavior of my family led me to a severe case of isolation and withdrawal. I was just a little boy who thought something was terribly wrong with him and that I was the root of all the problems my parents had. I became depressed at a very young age and nothing could hold my interests. I was just empty inside, but on the outside I wore a mask. A mask that portrayed a happy and content child who didn't even love himself, nor think anyone else did, how could they?

When I was five years old we lived out on an old farm southeast of Garnett, KS. A friend of my mom and dad was the school bus driver. I don't remember him very well, but after a lifetime of searching I have been able to identify the root of my problem. The individual I am speaking of is deceased now so I did not have the opportunity to forgive him in person. I was with him one day and I had to go to the bathroom. This is when he decided to take advantage of me in a sexual manner. After it was over with he told me to promise him that I wouldn't say anything to anyone. As you know, children are impressionable so I promised him that I wouldn't tell anyone.

I didn't know what to think, I just wanted to go home and never see this man again. Anytime this guy would come over I would run away from the house. I didn't want to be anywhere near him.

I was afraid he would do the same thing he did before. I am truly surprised that my parents didn't notice a difference in me. I just didn't understand why my parents liked this guy so much. It's a tragedy, but it happens each and every day in this world we live in. It can happen to anyone, there are no exceptions.

The second time it happened I was at work with my dad and a friend of mine was with us. I was nine at the time and he was eleven. We were playing cowboys and Indians like many little boys do and he caught me so he said let me tie your hands up to the pole. I let him and that is when he began to take advantage of me in a sexual way. I felt sick and disgusted. The shame I felt was so overwhelming that I just closed all doors. The humiliation devoured my light and left me lurking in the dark. I didn't know nor did I understand why I felt the way I did. A few years passed and the reason was revealed.

Summer was over and my seventh grade year was in session. About half way through health class we began to learn about human sexuality and the way things are between men and women. When I seen this I became silently outraged. I now understood what these two individuals were trying to accomplish with their actions. I became angry with myself because I didn't do anything when it happened. I held all of this in my heart for thirty five years before I told someone for the first time. I thank God everyday for that woman being placed in my life. The words this woman spoke to me made all the difference in the world. She said, Michael, it is important that you realize that you were only a child. Because you were a child you were helpless, it is not your responsibility. There was absolutely nothing you could do about it. Before this session was over I forgave myself and I forgave the other individuals involved. I felt instant relief. It was like a house being lifted from my chest. Today my heart is truly grateful for finding the courage and the trust to deal with these issues.

When school was in I did what I could but nothing we did could hold my interests. It was pretty boring for me, but most of the other children seemed to be enjoying themselves. I would learn what we were doing and then I would move on. I always thought what we did was just too simple so I didn't see any point in applying myself in that area. I felt I needed more of a challenge in my life, I just didn't know what it was. When I decided to do something I would just do it, didn't think about the consequences behind my actions. I felt alone, because of all the things I had been through I assumed that no one truly wanted to be around me. My way of thinking was distorted, no one knew what had happened to me. I made all of that up in my mind and that is how I lived the first 35 years of my life.

I am my mother's baby and she never truly disciplined me when I did something wrong. I would go out for hours and it was like I wasn't even missed. I felt as long as I was gone doing something and out of my mother's hair, she was happy. I had this yearning inside of me that I couldn't identify for many years. I just wanted some attention from my parents and I found out quickly the best way to get it was to act out and do something wrong. This desperate act helped when it came to my mother, she was there.

After I discovered this, I was on my way to being a juvenile delinquent. I began to break windows, shoplift what ever I felt I wanted at the time, and start fights with other children and try my best to hurt them. Why? Because I just wanted to be loved like any other child. I believe that everyone of us go through this at some point in our lives. We are only human and all of us want to feel loved by our parents. It's only natural.

Then that day came, I finally made it to the courtroom by the time I was 12 years old and put on probation for the first time. My mother came to the court proceedings with me and my father stayed at home. I expected this from him because he never went to anything that I was involved in as a child. It was routine and just the way it was, good or bad, it didn't matter. I was placed on probation a couple more times before reaching high school.

By the time my high school years rolled around I was drinking alcohol, smoking cigarettes, and partaking in a little marijuana. This behavior led to skipping school on a regular basis until I finally just dropped out my Junior year. After I quit I moved out of my mom and dad's house. I moved to Iola, KS where I got a job at a grocery store known as Greaves Nu-Way as a bag boy. It was a pretty cool job and I met some people that I ended up getting into trouble with. I was arrested for theft several times and thrown in the county jail until they would put me on probation again and I would promise the Judge that I would stay out of trouble.

I went to Allen County Community College and earned my GED which led to a scholarship. So I tried to attend classes their and get an Associates Degree in Business Communication. I had a girlfriend at the time and it went all bad so I dropped out of school and decided to go to the east coast. I learned the hard way that just because you move, your problems don't go away. I worked out there for three or four months, met a girl and moved back home to Garnett. After I returned to Garnett with the girl from Maryland my ex-girlfriend came back around to make amends. I of course fell for the entire charade, I felt in my heart that I loved her and it was the right thing to do. So I told the girl from Maryland, she understood and she went back without question. As soon as she was gone, my girlfriend broke up with me. She said that's what you get, you broke my heart. Shortly after that I began to date a girl that soon became my wife and the mother of my daughter that I haven't seen for almost ten years now. We were married for almost three years before she filed for a divorce. I lost my wife, my daughter, and my purpose for living all at once. I couldn't understand why my relationships continued to end in ruin. My heart was screaming and my mind was numb.

I had several scrapes with the law growing up and spent many nights in jail. When my wife and I got a divorce my life went completely south. I began drinking, doing drugs, and partying every night once again. I would go to work drunk and high and

I would get high while being at work. I was trying my hardest to forget what was going on around me. Low and behold, every time I opened my eyes the problem was still there. I couldn't deal with it, my heart was so empty. I felt I had been a failure my entire life and that I was going to be the best husband and the greatest dad, I knew that would fill the void I had in my heart.

I thought I had hit rock bottom, unfortunately I was wrong once again. My wife and I had talked on a few occasions and they never turned out very well. I thought I was right and she thought she was right. I had it in my head that we should put our daughter first so she would have both of her parents in her life. I learned later in life that it's not always the right choice, it could be worse on the child if you stay together. This really enraged me, I couldn't stand the fact that I had failed as a husband and as a father to the most precious little girl in the world.

As my life continued on a downward spiral, I went to her house one night and literally kicked the door in on her and demanded we be a family. I was doing it my way once again. My daughter came out of her room crying her little eyes out. I thank God everyday for that because she deflated me when I saw her. My whole world became still. I do not know what I would of done if she didn't appear when she did. I grabbed my ex-wife by her arm and yanked on it. What I did was wrong and I take complete responsibility for my actions. No woman deserves that type of treatment from anyone. I just wanted to be a family and be happy. It wasn't until years later that I realized that I was selfish and stubborn, simply because I wouldn't participate in getting help.

Later on I was arrested for aggravated kidnapping and assault and battery. I sat in jail and came down off all the drugs and didn't know exactly what had transpired. I went through the court proceedings and ended up with intense supervised probation which I ended up violating. I was arrested and put in front of the judge and sent to prison. Now I knew I hit rock bottom for real, it couldn't get any worse. I was sentenced to 13 months in the Kansas Department of Corrections.

Looking back I do believe she wanted it to work in the long run but I was so pre-occupied with drugs and alcohol that I didn't see it. I remember several different occasions when she asked me to go to church with her and my daughter but I was to busy working. I thought as long as I was providing what else do I need to do. I was absorbed in my work and I spent no time with them except before work and before bed. So I know God was speaking to me even then, I just chose to ignore him. It only makes sense, if you don't know him, how can you acknowledge him? It's been over ten years since I've seen them and I pray to God that one day they will forgive me. It's in his hands and I have nothing but respect for that.

The only thing I could think is I'm actually going to prison. Was I worried about my family, my friends, or even my daughter? The truth, absolutely not. All I could think about was where am I going to get some more methamphetamine. Literally, that is all I could think about. I just wanted to forget about everything that was going on in my life at the time. I truly didn't care what was happening to me and I didn't take anyone else's feelings into consideration either. I was in complete denial. I just wanted the life of myself to be over with, I was tired of the pain and the agony that came with all of my decisions. Sounds crazy, but it's true.

I sat in my cell day after day trying to grasp the fact that I am going to prison for real. I couldn't figure out what I did to deserve this type of treatment. This is just honesty people, I sincerely thought that everyone was just out to get me. My mind was completely absorbed in cognitive distortions and I deserved an explanation. I thought to myself, what else could possibly happen. After a couple of weeks in the county jail one of the jailors came up and gave me this phone number to call, that it was urgent. I made the call and the woman on the other end informed me that the best man in my wedding, my best friend was killed in an automobile accident the night before. I couldn't believe it man, this couldn't be true and I chose not to believe it because I didn't see it. It wasn't until almost seven years later that I wrote his ex-wife and asked her if it was true. I just didn't believe anything anyone told me. It was true.

I can say that I didn't love myself, and because I didn't love me, there was no way I could love anyone else. I thought I did, but my actions proved otherwise. I just kept telling myself to stop thinking about it and it would go away. Thirteen months isn't that long in prison. I sat in the county jail until September of 2000 until they put me in the car and transported me to RDU in Topeka, KS.

Otherwise known as the Radac Diagnostic Unit for the Kansas Department of Corrections. They keep you there long enough to run you through a battery of tests which determines a number of things. For example, what prison you will be going to, what custody level you will be starting out at, and what programs you should participate in while incarcerated whether it be drug treatment, GED, or literacy.

I spent two weeks in that facility and then they sent me to Hutchinson Correctional Facility. I will never forget the first time I saw the outside of this penitentiary. It was spooky, eerie, and looked like something out of mid evil times. It reminded me of some of the prisons I had seen on the television before. The only difference, this one was real and my temporary home for 13 months.

I went through A/D (admissions and discharge), got my picture taken, stripped out, and given a bed roll. After I was dressed I was told to put my things in the cart and follow the gentleman in front of me. His job was to show us the cell house we were going to be living in. I found my cell and it was with four other gentleman. They seemed like pretty decent people and we got to know each other until they moved me up to D2 cell house. This is a level one cell house which means no TVs or radios. People read and play a lot of cards in this cell house.

As I began to get settled in and learn the way around there I met a few guys that I started hanging around with on a regular basis. We walked the yard together, lifted weights together, and shot the breeze an awful lot. Still at this time all I could think about was getting my hands on some dope to escape this thing we call reality. Needless to say it happened and it became a regular part of my prison life. Honestly, it was no different than on the street. You can get anything that your heart desires in their if you have the resources and the right connections.

Suddenly, they called my name one day and said I needed to report to this certain room. I complied and when I got there it ended up being ADAPT, drug and alcohol treatment. This is the only program that I was to complete during my time in prison. This ended up being a big joke for real. I learned absolutely nothing in this program and that was my choice and no ones fault but my own. I didn't want the responsibility of it all and I wasn't ready to quit doing drugs in anyway, shape, or form. Drugs made me feel good and they helped me forget temporarily, that's all I had.

I honestly can't remember a lot about my first experience in prison. This may sound odd, however, one thing that I do remember like yesterday is a fellow convict telling me God can fill the void in your heart, nothing else can. I didn't know this man, never spoke to him before, and never saw him again. At that time, what did I do? I dismissed what he said because to me there was no God. I remember thinking, what kind of God would allow all this to happen to my family and to myself? I just didn't understand what he was talking about nor did I know anything about this God he was referring to. Later on I found out that this God he was referring to is as real as the air we breathe.

A few days later they told me to pack my belongings and go to A/D, you are going home. I truly didn't know how to feel about that. Why? Because I had no reason nor purpose for going back out their. I was so depressed, lost, and feeling so sorry for myself at the time that I didn't care what happened to me. I thought if there were a God, why doesn't he wave that wand and make everything better. I stood there waiting, yet nothing happened. I just wanted to scream at the top of my lungs, help me, please help me. My pride kept me from uttering a word, I continued with the philosophy that I could do it on my own, that I didn't need anyone.

I asked how much longer it would be before they were going to let me out and they said we're not, you have a detainer in Anderson County for a concealed weapon. The Sheriff's Department will be here shortly to take you back to the county jail. I was completely dumbfounded and didn't understand. I forgot that when I was arrested they found a blackjack in my back pocket. They considered it a concealed weapon so the sheriff at the time charged me with a class A misdemeanor.

As I sat in the county I knew I was only one step away from doing some meth. I couldn't wait so I began to think what would speed this process up and get me out of here. When I was in Hutchinson I did take some time to learn a little about the law. So I found me a piece of paper and wrote a motion for sentence modification to the Judge. I sent it to him and next thing you know I had a court date to hear the motion. I had already been in the county for ninety days and only had ninety to go so it wouldn't hurt to try. The judge honored the motion and I was released from the jail. Myself, I couldn't believe it, it worked.

I was to go to my mom and dad's house and figure out what I was going to do. Unfortunately I didn't make it that far. Not an hour upon my release I had an eight ball of meth in my pocket and hanging out with the same fellas I hung with before I went to prison. I remember thinking to myself that it just doesn't get any better than this, and deep down inside I asked myself what in the world are you doing to your family and yourself Michael. What is wrong with you? Are you totally insane, do you remember where you just came from and what got you their? Wake up stupid, you are doing it all over.

My friend got me a job working with him digging up telephone cable and replacing it. It was an interesting job and I liked the guys that I worked with. We had one thing in common, we all liked to do drugs. So we worked and we did drugs whenever we wanted to. For some reason I could never do enough. I come to realize I was on a self destruct mission and just had to much pride to ask anyone for help. I was just so sick and tired of my life, but I didn't want to do anything to make it better.

Nothing had changed, and that little 13 months I did in prison did no good. Honestly, it was just a vacation from where I was before. It was just an introduction of what was soon coming my way. Before I knew it I was hanging around some other people I did drugs with before and began to miss work here and there. It was the same old routine as before except I reached that point much quicker. I would drink and do drugs all night and go to work the next day. I thought I was doing a good thing, at least I was showing up and doing my job. To me it was all good. I believed that because no one at work said anything to me about it. However, my mom and dad did voice their concerns, but I dismissed them as quick as they said them. I knew what I was doing and no one could tell me any different.

I remember one day me and my mother had a talk and she had mentioned she knew I was severely depressed and that she thought I should go see some one about it. She knew this doctor that would prescribe me some anti-depressant medication and that would be the cure to all of my problems. I thought about it for a while and decided to honor her plea. The doctor put me on what they refer to as Paxil. I thought what could it hurt. At the same time I wasn't willing to give up doing the drugs even if I was taking this medication. It just didn't matter to me. So I continued to do the same thing along with the Paxil. At first I didn't know if I was just tripping or if the alcohol, meth, and Paxil was having more of an adverse effect upon me. So what did I do? I just ignored it and continued down that path. My thinking became even more distorted.

Honestly, I never felt so lost in my life. I couldn't concentrate at work, I drank more and more, I used more drugs, and distanced myself farther away from my family than before. I became desperate at the end by acting out unlike before. Desperate pleas for help if you will and I'm sure many of you can identify with this type of behavior. I began treating my parents with no respect, I neglected all my responsibilities, tried to overdose on narcotics, and tried to commit suicide by swallowing pills. Why did I do this you may ask? All I can tell you is pride, and self pity. My pride was so deeply rooted that it was slowly suffocating me and at the same time my family. However, my selfishness kept me in the blind. I truly thought that if I'm the one all of this is happening to, how could they be emotionally shaken. It was beyond me and as long as I was self medicated it didn't exist.

I soon began to stay away from home after work hanging out with a couple of old friends drinking, doing meth, and just having what I called a good time. It wasn't long before I noticed that the drug meth had many advantages to it when it came to other people. To this day I am still amazed by the power this drug can have over someone as if they were hypnotized. It's like Jeckyl and Hyde, no exaggeration. It becomes a tool of manipulation to get what you want, and the more you practice this and get away with it, the more courage it gives you to push the envelope. Once the drug slowly strips you of what will power you have and consumes every ounce of strength that you possess you have two choices. You can continue on a downward spiral by relying on your own strength, or you can just say that you are sick and tired of being sick and tired. I would like to share a few words of wisdom with you if you are currently suffering from any type of addiction in your life. Do not rely on your own understanding because that is what got you where you are today. Please, relax, open your mind and allow someone to help you, guide you, and direct you during your time of need.

It wasn't long before I became a true slave to methamphetamine. I loved this drug more than my own life. My wife and daughter gave me the greatest feeling I have ever felt in my heart and I took for granted that they would always be their. The day they were gone it went from one extreme to the other. My heart was dark and empty. The only thing that I ever found that filled that void and gave me the same feeling was methamphetamine. So I told myself I found the answer to my own problem. Like any other temporary fix in life this one is notorious for slowly breaking down all of our healthy boundaries. It does it at such a slow pace that you don't even notice it, you become it. A friend may point a change out in your behavior or your morals and you become defensive, true denial. This couldn't happen to me and I wouldn't allow that to happen. Your thoughts become distorted, your judgment deteriorates quickly, and all inhibitions are lost. It is a viscous cycle that could eventually lead to death unless intervention happens and that's real.

Every night after work I would go over to a friends house and just kick it. We would sit around and drink beer, smoke weed, shoot and smoke meth, and listen to music all night long. It was routine for me to look out the window and see daylight once again. Time for me to go to work and do it all over again. After work I would go back over to his house. My friend had his problems, but I always liked the dude. His teenage daughter lived with him at the time and she was a cool girl. I knew her for awhile, however, I didn't know much about her until I started hanging around the house with her dad.

One night we were sitting out in the living room and she came out and joined us. We were having casual conversation, drinking beer, and smoking weed. Next thing I know her dad hands her the joint and she's hitting this thing like a champ. We were all high and we continued to get higher and just talk crazy to one another. At this point in time I don't even know why I was smoking the weed because I had already been up for almost a week on meth. Just something to do at the time. As the days went by I did notice a difference in the way she was acting towards me. I can honestly say that she was flirting with me and instead of me being a responsible adult at the time and telling her what she was doing was inappropriate I kept my mouth shut.

This type of thing happens to people all the time. If you already suffer from any type of emotional problem and then you mix it with drugs you are in truly bad shape. At the time I didn't know it, but there is only one who can help you overcome this self-destructive behavior. The answer is the one true living God. I thank God for

His grace and mercy, because without Him we would all be in serious trouble. There would be not hope. So if you are in an abyss, I encourage you to lay your pride down and ask God to lift you up. Do not put limits on God, there is nothing He can not do in your life only if you ask Him. I found out that with God all things are possible regardless who you are. He loves you and He delights in you for you are His creation and He created you with a great purpose.

It's now January and it's cold out. Nothing has really changed in my life, same old bump and grind. Work is work, I show up and do what they ask of me. The day is January 8, 2002, my momma's birthday. I was looking forward to this night because some of my family was coming over for dinner and to spend time with mom. We all just sat down to eat when the door was knocked on. Mom opened it up and it was the Franklin County Sheriff's Department. They asked her if her son Michael Teter was there and she said yes, why? They said we have a warrant for his arrest out of Anderson County for rape and aggravated kidnapping. She said you must be mistaking, they came in and told me what was going on and I asked them if I could get a few things. Of course they wouldn't let me out of their sight because I am known for taking off on them. They cuffed me and put me in the car.

This was truly the lowest time of my life. Imagine your family all gathered together to celebrate the birthday of your mother. Your mom and dad are their, your sister, her husband and their three little girls, my nieces. The look on their faces when the police walked into the house to place me under arrest. The shame and embarrassment that I felt was overwhelming, they were just staring at me in disbelief. I can't even imagine what was going through their minds, probably something to this measure. Michael, you just got out of prison not three months ago, what are you thinking. I couldn't even look at them and tell them how sorry I was. It was just routine and they may of been thinking the same thing.

The next day they transported me to the county line and the Anderson County Sheriff's Department took me to the jailhouse where a long process began. I soon went in front of the Judge and he laid it all out on the table for me. He explained that if I was convicted of all of the charges I could be sentenced to 33 years in prison and up to 66 years if the statute allows the doubling rule. I was oblivious to everything this man said, I didn't care about anything long before this. I went back to my cell until the next court hearing. They appointed an attorney to my case and I met with him on several occasions. He spoke with the prosecution and they struck up a plea bargain agreement. The prosecution was willing to drop all of those charges that I was being accused of to a class A misdemeanor. Myself, I couldn't believe that. I asked myself why is the prosecution willing to drop a rape charge all the way down to a misdemeanor.

My attorney encouraged me at the time to take the deal and I would only do a year in the county jail. I thought about it for awhile and decided to comply with his wishes. Shortly after that we went to court to finalize the plea and the prosecution withdrew the original deal from the table. My attorney filed a motion and it was shot down. After that I went back to my cell waiting for my attorney to come see me and inform me on our next move. The next time I saw my attorney I told him I would like to take a polygraph test before this goes any further. He informed me that it wasn't necessary. Once again I took his advice and rolled with the punches.

The Anderson County Jail was a small jailhouse. I was upstairs and the max capacity was 14 inmates. I was in their for nine months and I never seen it full one time. Being the small county that it was, almost everyone that came in the jail I knew from the streets. We would sit around and play cards, watch TV, read books, and smoke cigarettes. The nice thing about this place is that they would give you squares if you didn't have any in your property. They would take you outside four times a day to smoke. That was really cool of them because they didn't have to let you smoke. You couldn't of asked for better jailors. I went to high school with one of them, one was the dad of a friend, and the rest I knew from just being in a small town.

The time was going by slowly and my attitude kept changing for the worse. I didn't know what was going to happen and I felt like I was about to explode. I woke up one day and I couldn't even spell the word hope. I was lost and to the point of no return. The feeling of uncertainty is overwhelming, fear consumes your heart, and darkness creeps up on you from nowhere. It can become your reality if you allow it, or you can rise above the circumstances taking charge of your life. It's a tough decision to make when you are incarcerated, your pride is at stake. Pride is sin and we all know that sin leads to death. Proverbs 11:2 NLT-Pride leads to disgrace, but with humility comes wisdom. New Living Translation.

The county brought in a couple farm outs from Lynn County one day and they seemed like descent individuals. One inmate began to talk to me and I could tell that he was truly proud of what he did and he wanted everyone to know about it. After he made it known he settled down for the most part and we became pretty good friends. He was 19 years old and thought being in jail was the greatest thing going. One night we all decided to smoke some weed and after the fact he told us that it was his first time doing so. He began to act crazy and started talking down to all of us including the jailors. I just told myself to let it go and we would talk to him about it later when he was calmer.

We all went to sleep that night feeling pretty good. Next thing I know they were calling breakfast and everyone got up to eat. I sat across from the dude who was talking crazy to everyone. I was just minding my own when out of nowhere this guy called me out of my name. That was it for me, I had had enough of his arrogant attitude towards people in his own situation. I had a full pint of milk in my hand when I stood up and smashed it into his face. I hit him square in the chin and it was curtains. He fell backwards and when his head met the concrete he awoke. He laid there with a vacant look on his face. I told him to get up and square up. He got up, but he didn't want anymore. I didn't give him a choice. When I went after him he ran so I chased him down and finished what he started.

It's the next day when the jailor comes up to give us a smoke break. As we get outside the jailor notices that this dude has a swollen up face. I hear him ask the fella what happened to him and I couldn't make out what he said to him. Later that night dude was writing a letter at the table and I asked him what he was doing because he appeared to be nervous. He said he was writing his dad a letter and I said cool, don't forget to tell him about your first ass whooping. He got up from the table and put the letter in the mailbox like normal inmate procedure. I didn't know I was in for such a surprise. The letter he put in the mailbox had to the jailor written on it.

The following evening we are playing a card game when five or six deputies come up to the cell block. I knew something wasn't right and they proceeded to say Teter cuff up. I said what for and one of the deputies said we are transporting you to Neosho County. I said for what reason. His response, you are in need of isolation. They put me in the car and we drove off for my new destination. I went straight to segregation. A one man cell and I had the entire pod to myself. This was it, I couldn't take it any longer. I just wanted to end it all, let this night mare be over with already. I evaluated my cell and soon found the solution. I stripped the bunk and found a sheet. I made it into a noose and tied it to the light fixture. I placed it around my neck and went limp. I felt my throat constricting and the oxygen flow to my brain slowly dissipate. I was slipping into a darkness I would never return from.

I was finally relaxing when something told me to take one last look around me. I opened my eyes and right before me on the floor was a picture, backside facing up. It read, I love you daddy. My heart started racing like never before and my calmness became a panic. I forgot what my purpose at the time was and during my struggle for life I accidentally hit the intercom button which was on the wall in front of me. My instincts took over at this point in time. I woke up in this cell with only three other things. My boxer shorts, the mattress, and The Holy Bible. I said to myself what kind of joke is this, I'm alive and I'm elated at the same time.

It wasn't long after I woke up that a jailor came into the isolation, observation room to talk to me. I asked her what was going on and why I'm in this cell with all of the windows in it. She said this is where we put people who are a threat to themselves. I know to this day that they believe that I was just seeking attention, also known as a desperate cry for help, she told me this herself. I didn't tell her anything different, but I will tell you the truth. The truth is that it wasn't a desperate cry for help. I was just sick and tired of being sick and tired. I thank God everyday for that intercom button in my cell. The simple truth is that sin leads to death, it will consume you if you continue to let your pride rule your life.

I am truly grateful for that experience because it was God working in my life and I didn't even know it. The Bible was laying on the floor next to my bunk for quite awhile before I could finally swallow my pride and open it up. At this point in time I had no understanding what the book was even about. I flipped through it until I came to the New Testament, the Book of Matthew. I began to read and I found the story pretty intriguing. I continued to read until I was finished with Matthew. Next came Mark, I read it as well. I thought to myself, I don't get this. These two books are almost identical to one another. I thought that was weird, I didn't understand why two books in a row read almost word for word.

I dismissed the thought and began to read the Book of Luke. Wouldn't you know it, the same result. I thought to myself that there is a logical explanation for all of this. My journey continued into the Book of John and it proved to be the same as well. I became pretty interested in these stories and read them all several times looking for a difference in them. While I was involved doing this a friend of mine walked through the door where the police book people in. This may sound crazy but it's the truth, he talked them into letting me out of that isolation cell and placing me into the same pod with him. He told them he would keep an eye on me. I thought that was admirable of my friend.

About an hour passed and they let me out of the isolation cell. I moved into B pod, four man cell. My cellies included my partner and two young fellas. It was pretty interesting from the jump. My friend and I started playing spades for breakfast trays because they do not feed you anything in their. We were doing well for ourselves and one day we sat down to play these two fellas from Johnson County and things went south. It was their turn to deal so dude shuffled the cards. He put them in front of me to cut and I said deal them. He grabbed them up and did this quick little move with his hand and began to pass them out. When he was finished I ended up with the last card so I called a misdeal. The dealer is suppose to get the last card and he didn't.

After I called misdeal he copped an attitude. So we asked several gentlemen and they also said it was a misdeal. He got all in his feelings and said he didn't want to play anymore. I said cool, give me my five dollars and were done. He declined to honor his word and now I copped an attitude. I found out why he got upset. When he dismissed himself from the table my bro flipped his cards over and he had every spade in the deck except two of them. When he told me this I went to his cell and I confronted him about it causing him to become enraged. It was a funny sight, really dramatic. I just said check this out, give me my money and I'm out of here and it's all over. He wouldn't pay me so I told him to stand up so we could settle this situation. He got up and we fought it out. When it was over he gave me my five dollars and admitted he was in the wrong and I respected him for that. That took a lot of courage to do in front of several other gentlemen.

The days passed by slowly and we became bored because no one wanted to play anymore cards. So we decided to make some hooch in our cell. It was going pretty good and some how the police found out about it and they bum rushed our living quarters. When the search was complete, they came out with a couple gallons of drink.

I was disappointed for real because it was only one day from being done. We were going to drink a little bit and just kick back and relax. Nothing came of it except they moved my bro out of the cell and down stairs to a one man cell.

The next day they brought in a farm out from Lynn County. My bro being from Lynn County knew this fella. It was pretty obvious they didn't get along. One day while sitting out in the day room my bro asked dude what was going on up north. He was honestly trying to be peaceful with the other fella, but he wasn't having that. His response, I don't have anything to say to you so fly away. They ended up getting into a fight. Bro went postal on dude, he had no clue where he was when it was all over. The police ran in the pod and pulled bro off dude and locked him in his cell. They tried to calm him down, but one of the cops, this young dude actually hit him when they pulled them apart.

At this point in time bro looks like a wild bull in that little cell. The police kept talking to him and he became more upset as they did this. Then came their bright idea of rushing him in his cell. When they did this he ended up breaking one of their noses and they beat him up pretty good. The crazy thing about it is that it took six of them to do it. He ended up with a couple broken ribs and a fractured ankle. It was nothing nice to see. When all of this was going down I didn't know whether to jump in the middle of it or watch them beat him up. Later on when I seen him again he said I did the right thing. That made me feel much better about the situation.

Now with bro being in the hole everything was pretty boring around B pod. I was sitting out in the day room one day reading a letter. A ladies voice came over the intercom telling us to lockdown because the day room was now closed. Someone in the pod yelled shut up. I was minding my own business when she said Teter go to your cell and pack your things, you are going to the hole. I disagreed with her, I asked her what I was going to the hole for. She said for disrespecting me. I asked, how did I disrespect you? She said you called me a horrible name. Therefore, I will show you. We all went to our cells and they locked the doors.

About an hour passed and this dude asked me over the intercom if I had my things ready. I said for what and he said for the hole. I started laughing out loud, I couldn't believe this was going down. I just said check this out dude, if you want me to go to the hole you can come get my stuff ready and take me to the hole if you can. Ten minutes later my door popped open and there were five jailors outside my cell door. House, the head jailor asked me to go peacefully and I said I did nothing to bring this on. He even agreed with me, that was his mistake. I said if you know this then do your job and say something about it. He said he already tried and she isn't trying to hear it.

I couldn't believe this was actually transpiring at this time. All I could say is if you are going to make my job hard then I will do the same for you. He said are you resisting and I said but of course. He got on his radio and had the people clear all of the cells out and send them to the wreck room. One of my cellies offered to stay but I told him to burnout. When everyone else was clear I seen fear in their eyes as they were about to embark upon a hostile situation. My adrenaline began to shoot through my veins like ice water. I could feel the anticipation getting closer and closer so I put my back to the wall. This is the best thing you can do when you are about to fight more than four people.

They rushed me and the fight was on, it lasted about two minutes tops. They were cussing up a storm and using their authority to make a point. I couldn't let them have the satisfaction of defeating me so I let them know that it would be a different story if they would fight me one on one. They said nothing. They pushed my face into the concrete floor, cuffed my hands behind my back, and cuffed my ankles to my hands. This is what they refer to as hog tying someone. They drug me out the door, down the stairs, and used my head to open the double doors to the pod. It felt really good I must tell you. Next stop, D pod, back in the hole again. They threw me in the cell face down and that is the last thing I saw until I regained consciousness.

When I woke up I couldn't even feel my arms because they were numb from lack of circulation. I worked my way over to the wall and managed to hit the button to the intercom with my head. The voice that answered was familiar, it was her, the one who claimed that I called her a horrible name. She asked me what the problem was and I told her I couldn't feel my arms so they sent a few guys in their. When the cell door opened the Sergeant couldn't believe his eyes. The fact that I was still in handcuffs and hog tied set him off. He knew they had taken me to the hole on the prior shift, but didn't know they left me in restraints. They undid the cuffs and jumped out of the cell. The Sergeant looked in and asked if I understood any of this. I began to laugh out loud as the darkness devoured my spirit. The last words that I heard before I slipped back into the world of unconsciousness was you can be forgiven.

Several hours had passed before I woke up. First thing that came to my mind was the words the Sergeant shared with me about forgiveness. I contemplated those words for several minutes before I decided to dismiss them completely. Sadly, I didn't even like myself, who would forgive me. That is how I minimized and justified the entire situation. Besides, I was heading to prison for a decade or longer and I couldn't go in their being some soft ass dude. I was on a mission and I was more than determined to accomplish it. I was living in a dark place at this time with no hopes of seeing daylight anytime soon.

A few weeks had transpired before they decided to allow me back into general population. They told me to get my personal belongings together and be ready when the door opens. Well, the door opened so I walked through it and followed the officer in charge to my new destination. They told me what cell to go to and I did as they asked. A couple hours later one of the jailors asked me if I would like to be one of the pod porters. I thought this was their idea of a sick joke. I have wreaked nothing but havoc in their facility and now they would like for me to be one of the trustees. I ran this through my mind several times and I couldn't make sense out of it. I knew they had an ulterior motive behind this entire situation or they wouldn't be asking me to do this. After the day was over I informed them that I would accept their offer and be one of the trustees.

Being a trustee has a few benefits and it has a few downfalls. The benefits include extra time out of your cell, extra food, and some coffee here and there. The downfalls are simply listening to the other inmates call you names and make fun of you for accepting this type of job. At the same time you know in your heart that if they were offered the position they would jump on it as well so you just ignore the peanut gallery altogether. As I was cleaning up one day I ran into this young man who was looking at approximately seven years in the joint. I have never seen anyone so terrified in my life.

Since I had been to prison once already I tried to give this young man some peace in his heart. It wasn't long before I realized that I wasn't getting through to him. I didn't know what else to do and that afternoon he asked me to sit down. I sat down at the table he was holding down. I said what's on your mind kid. He looked at me with the most confused look I have ever seen in my entire life. He said not much, it's the end of the road. I said no, it's just the beginning for you kid, you're young and you will still be young when you get out. You can have a fresh start at life and do whatever you set your mind to. He said no, it's over and walked away from the table.

They brought the lunch cart in and everyone grabbed their tray and ate. After all the inmates are finished they lock the pod down while the trustees clean the day room and place the cart outside of the pod. When the day room is finished they open the day room back up and the inmates wander back to it. This overwhelming feeling came to life in my mind and I couldn't shake it. This voice told me to watch for the kid over and over. I looked up at his door as he came through it and I seen a noose around his neck. I immediately ran for the stairs as he was tying the noose to the railing. Talk about just in time, as he jumped over the railing I caught his left arm just below the elbow. I thank God to this day that he was only 5'6" tall and weighed no more than 130lbs. Why? Because I had the size and the strength to keep him from falling to his death. It wasn't easy by any means, this little dude was determined to die. He fought harder than anyone I have ever fought in a regular physical confrontation.

I was holding him while he was screaming at the top of his lungs let me go, just let me go please. I couldn't allow this kid to go out like that, he had to much to give in this life. I got him almost over the top of the rail and he just fought harder. I didn't know if I was going to get him back on the safe side or not. Everything became slow motion; his words, his swinging at me, and all the movement around me. I seen an opening so I took it. I quickly wrapped my arms around his torso while using every bit of strength I could summon to pull him back to the runway. We landed on the floor and he was still trying to hit me. I didn't know what to do at this point so I followed my instinct. I clenched my fist and hit him on the chin with everything I had. It was curtains, he was out of it and that gave me the opportunity to untie the sheet from the railing.

As I was doing that the police ran up on me like I had done something wrong. They soon realized what had transpired. All of the other inmates just stood where they were giving me the most disturbed looks. I said what, what's up. One of them popped off and said he wanted to die, you should of just let him hang. Another one said I won't get involved in anything like that, I don't know any of you. I said wow, if I remember correctly almost everyone of you have told me how rough and tough you are. I disagree, everyone of you are nothing but a coward with no respect for human life. I couldn't stand there any longer, my heart was truly disgusted. I went to my cell seeking some type of solace and understanding behind all of this hate and discontent.

I heard someone saying my name, it was like an echo. I was half asleep when I felt the presence of people in my cell. I opened my eyes and it was the sheriff of Neosho County. First thing that came to my mind is that he thinks I had something to do with the prior incident involving the kid. I sat up and he told me he would like to talk to me for a minute or two if I don't mind. I said go ahead, speak your piece then leave me be. He said he was truly grateful for doing what I did earlier involving the kid. He continued to explain to me that the facility that we are now in is brand new. He said since the doors opened one man has successfully taken his own life by hanging himself. Furthermore, it has brought a lot of negative energy along with bad press our way involving this facility. I said I didn't do what I did because I was concerned about your precious facility, I did it because he is a human being. He said I see, we have a man of compassion on board here. You have a good day Mr. Teter and thank you.

I still don't know what to think about what the sheriff said that day. I feel a little unsettled in my heart about the entire situation. I believe he was being sarcastic about me being a man of compassion and that's cool. People say things like that when they do not have the courage to step up to the plate. I didn't know that at the time, but I know that now. It is really sad if you think about it. This man is an authority figure who was more concerned about the new facility that just opened rather than the kid who just fought tooth and nail to take his own life. I just took the entire conversation with a grain of salt, what can you do. I'm elated to this day that this young man was not successful. I have a good feeling that he is doing well and living life to the fullest. That is a blessing for real.

I went about my days in Neosho County with a different outlook on life. After that experience I believe I began to contemplate the true meaning of life. I kept it to myself, however I felt hopeless at the same time. I knew in a few short days I would be traveling back to Anderson County to be sentenced to the Kansas Department of Corrections, for how long? Only God knows. I had absolutely no control over the situation. My fate was sealed. I knew in my heart that once I arrived at the facility I would never walk out of it. I truly believed that in the deepest part of my heart. Once again as you can see I was wrong. Someone had a different plan for me, and to this day I am so grateful.

Me and my cellies would pass the time by playing cards, playing chess, and just talking about life. We would sit up till the early morning hours telling each other what we would be doing on the outside if we weren't in here right now. Needless to say, we all were up to no good. We would be out partying, doing drugs, and drinking the brew until we all fell out. That sounds completely ludicrous to this day. I look back at all the times I did this exact thing and ask myself what were you thinking. The answer to my question is simple, I was just throwing a pity party for myself. We all go through it at some point in our lives because we are only human. We are not perfect by any means, it is human nature to experience these trials and tribulations. I wish I knew this back then, maybe things would of been different. I wouldn't be the man I am today if it were different and that I'm grateful for.

The lights came on and the trustee brought the breakfast cart into the pod. The doors snapped open and the residents of B pod slowly wandered toward the aroma of jail house French toast. Now this is something to talk about if you know what I mean. Nothing can compare to the sight of twenty six men who have no idea what is going to happen to them. It was almost like watching zombies, men with no purpose in life. It is sad but we all make our own decisions. What you decide to do about the poor decisions you make is the question. You can either continue down the same path of no hope or you can be redeemed. It's your choice, no one can do it for you.

Shortly after breakfast a voice is heard on the intercom. All I heard is Teter, get your things together, you are going to court. I thought cool, I get to go for a ride fellas. It's going to be a good day. Once you have your freedom taken away sooner or later you begin to recognize all of the things you have taken for granted. I got my things together and the sheriff's deputy came and cuffed me up. He took me to the garage and placed me in the cruiser. They pulled out and we were on our way to good ole Garnett, KS. My home town, my stomping grounds. A place where I have been part of many good and bad memories.

The ride there seemed like forever and a day. This was the day I have been waiting for. I would be going in front of Judge Smith for my sentencing. I had absolutely no clue how this was going to go. All I knew at the time is that my attorney and the DA made a deal of one year in the county jail. Out of all honesty I thought that was to good to be true so I had been preparing myself for the worst case scenario. When we arrived at Anderson County jailhouse I felt a sense of relief, it was my home and I knew everyone. They took me inside and put me in the drunk tank downstairs. When I got in front of the gate, my friend moose was sitting in the tank as well. I had no idea why, but now I think it was the jailors just being descent to me. I got along with most of them. I can say this, if you ever go to jail, Anderson County is the place to be. The staff is kind and understanding to all. They have a tremendous amount of compassion and they take pride in that. I thank all of you for your hospitality and kindness.

Moose and I chopped it up for about thirty minutes before they came and got me. It was really good to see him and he made me feel pretty good about the entire situation. The police cuffed me up and took me away. Right then and there I knew this would be the last time I would ever see him. After I got outside the bars I just looked at him and said be good bro, you know what you need to do. He just said take care of yourself my friend and we left. It was a long walk to the courthouse. My heart was racing and a thousand different scenarios were running through my mind like wild fire. I seen the big doors on the front of the courthouse just standing still, yet anxious for me to walk through them so they could devour my soul for the last time.

As I entered the courtroom all eyes were on me. It took every bit of strength I had left in my body, and the persuasive touch of the jailors to make it to my seat where my attorney awaited patiently. I focused on him with all of my energy, our eyes locked until I sat down next to him. He was being apprehensive which told me he didn't really want to be the one telling me what he had to say. He talked to the prosecutor and they agreed upon a pretty good deal, but it didn't sound to promising.

I just sat there patiently waiting for Judge Smith to say State vs. Teter. It was the longest waiting period I have ever endured. Seemed like an eternity. State vs. Teter, my attorney and I stood up, the prosecutor stood up. The proceedings began. Both parties made their argument and the judge said thank you. Then he asked me if I understood what was going on and if I knew that even though my attorney and the prosecutor had entered into a plea agreement that he didn't have to agree with it. I said yes your honor. The deal as I mentioned before was a year in the county jail. The judge said after looking over all of the facts and circumstances concerning my case that he didn't feel that one year in the county jail was a sufficient sentence. Therefore Mr. Teter I sentence you to 100 months in the Kansas Department of Corrections. The inmate will remain in the county jail until he can be transferred to state's custody. Court adjourned.

Honestly, I was overwhelmed not to mention speechless about the entire situation that day. I knew in my heart that I would be going to prison for quite sometime. I was correct about the matter at hand. They snatched me up and took me back to my cell. Not long after that a car was there to take me back to Neosho County jail. Talk about a long journey, this is the last time I would see anything familiar to me in a long time. I have never been away from home for this amount of time. I looked at everything as it passed by trying to savor the moment while the thread of purpose slipped away. I asked myself what else is there?

I felt the patrol car slow down as it turned into our destination point once again. It came to a rest in the garage and the door was opened. They escorted me inside the station and told me I would remain here until the arrangements with the KDOC are taken care of. As they escorted me back to the pod where I was staying at the time I felt all eyes upon me. It was like the end of the road; no energy, no understanding, and no sense of direction. Condemnation has become my new home. I am on my own for real, that is the most terrifying feeling a human being could ever endure. It is an entire different world and I pray that you will never experience it. It is a long journey, but it can be done. What doesn't kill you only makes you stronger and that is the truth.

I remember walking into the pod and several different people asked me what happened at court. I was bombarded with questions and smart remarks. I told a couple of the fellas that I was going to prison for quite a while. They had nothing to say about it except keep the faith alive and I said I have no faith. Faith is nonexistent and where I'm going you'll see that faith has no business being mentioned. I went to my cell where I penned my mother a letter telling her how I wish it could of been different. I really didn't know what else to say because I thought that she didn't love me anymore. I brought a lot of heartache and pain to her and my pops, yet they never gave up on me. I thank God to this day for giving me the parents that he chose for me, they are the best.

Dinner rolled around that night and we all sat down to eat. My cell mate asked me what I was going to do while being in prison. I said it doesn't matter what I do because I don't care if I ever walk out of it. He couldn't believe I said that, yet wanted to know why I said it. I said look dude, I love dope more than my own family. I chose it over them, I lost my wife, my daughter and they were the whole world to me. I was a complete failure, I failed my family, all of my friends, it was all over. Deep in my heart I knew my wife never truly loved me, she was just the mother of my little girl. However, I loved her more than life and that is what made it truly complex for me. To love someone so much and know they don't love you, I didn't know what to do about the situation. I kept telling myself that one day it may be different. I was gone, I thought she was the only woman in this entire world. Boy, was I ever so wrong and truly grateful that I was.

The night was growing shorter and it was time to lock down. I was lying in my bunk when this youngster asked me if there was a God. Talk about pressure, what do you do in a situation like this. I answered the best of my ability and told him no. Look where you're at kid, would God put your ass in here just to let you rot away? I think not, what did I know about this God thing. Not a thing and didn't care to either. The way I seen it is that you must be a weak minded individual if you need someone other than yourself to take care of business. I called it the easy way out and so do the majority in prison. Now I know why many of us go to prison, we tend to take things into our own hands instead of letting God handle the situation.

To this day I don't think I did that kid any good. I wish it could of been different now, but it happened that way for a reason. Maybe I'll see him again one day, it is a small world. The lights went out and the kid said something out of the side of his neck. I said what did you say, he said, you are a good person. You have helped me quite a bit without even knowing it. I said shut up and go to sleep before your mom comes in here and yells at you. He was relentless people, he said you'll see one day and when you do you will be a happy man. I think about this quite often because this kid was only 19 at the time and quite intuitive. I am a truly happy person today, almost eleven years later and that night continues to pop into my head. How could he have known that. I'm living it right now, the kid was dead on. I do not understand how he knew, but he did. I drifted into a deep sleep until the next morning.

Directly after breakfast the jailor told me to pack my belongings that it was my day. I said my day for what. He said you are going to El Dorado my friend. Wow! That was quick I said to myself. They didn't waste anytime getting me out of there. After you are sentenced to prison you usually have to wait for the KDOC to verify bed space and at the time the correctional facilities were so overcrowded the bed space was hard to come by. I guess they made an exception for me. About an hour later I got into the car with a couple jailors from Andersons county and was on the way to my new home for the next decade. Talk about a long ride, however, I managed to enjoy the scenery even though it wasn't all that. I knew this was the last time that I would be able to just look at everything I took for granted. It was all slowly slipping away while the new world of iron, guard towers, and concrete block were becoming more visible.

When we pulled up to El Dorado I couldn't believe all of the checkpoints that we had to go through just to get inside. After we reached our destination I was let out of the car and the jailors that escorted me told me good luck Michael and take care of yourself. I thought that was descent of them to say that to me. When I got inside they asked me my name, what county I'm from, etc. After they got all of the information required they put me in a two man cell. Like I mentioned before, I went to the RDU in Topeka the first time I went to prison. This was the new facility, it just opened up, the reason being is because they renovated the old RDU into the women's prison.

The two facilities are like night and day. They put you in a red two piece suit and give you a pair of bob barker shoes to wear around. You are locked down twenty three hours of every day. The idea behind this is to figure out the best place for you to go when you are released into general population. You are required to go through a series of testing and physical examinations to determine your mental and physical health status. When you have completed all of these requirements you just set in your cell and wait for the bus to take you to the prison you are going to go to. This may sound crazy to some people, but it is a happy day when they come and tell you that you are on the bus in the morning. At this point of incarceration you can only read, write, and tell the same lies so many times. That is just the truth.

My day came around and they told me I was going to Ellsworth Correctional Facility. I thought Ellsworth, I've never even heard of Ellsworth and this dude said it is way out in the middle of nowhere, he was absolutely correct. The longest bus ride of my life. It is located out in Western Kansas, not to far from Salina if you know where that is. The bus took off from El Dorado and we went through the township. I thought it was kind of odd because the people would stop and look, it was like they knew we were on our way to a completely different world. All the fellas on the bus were looking out the windows with the most vacant expressions I have ever witnessed during my entire life. It was like the reality of it all just set in, they were watching the world disappear as the bus slowly exited the township. Myself, I experienced that feeling on the way to El Dorado.

The bus ride was a long and quiet ride. It really gave you time to think about what you were about to face. You could actually smell the fear on that bus, however, if you were to ask someone if they were scared they would tell you absolutely not, I fear nothing. All the evidence is in their eyes and their voice. The men on the bus were all different ethnicities; black, white, Hispanic, and Asian. Some could speak English and some couldn't. I couldn't even imagine that. Knowing that you are going to prison is bad enough, but not being able to speak the language that everyone else is would be overwhelming. The age ranged from 17 to 65 years old. The simple truth was lying ahead all wrapped in several layers of razor wire.

There was an older gentleman on the bus and to me he seemed kind of mysterious in a good way. I didn't know what it was at the time, but I know what it was now. He was speaking to a younger man about the penitentiary. The younger fella was assaulting him with an arsenal of questions. The old man would start out by laughing, then he would begin reassuring him that he had nothing to be worried about. I thought that was really admirable of him to help that youngster find some sort of peace in all that madness. I know at some point in time I heard him say just trust in the Lord son, with him you will walk out a new man. When I heard that I just turned my head, and tried to tune out the conversation. I said to myself, not another one of theses guys. Why would he sell this young man a pipe dream, telling him to trust in something that you obviously can't see. I never heard of anything so ridiculous, the Lord is going to make everything so much better for this young man.

As the bus continued to roll down the empty highway all I could think about was my mom, my dad, and my little girl. I had no idea how long it would be, or if I would ever see them again. The memories flooded my mind once again, and all I could think is what if. What if none of this ever happened, where would I be. The only answer I came up with is probably dead. I'm not sure exactly how many times I escaped my own demise in process of my self destruction stage. It didn't matter what I tried during any hour of desperation. The end result was always the same, failure.

The bus began to slow down and in the distance I could see something that resembled a college campus only it was surrounded with razor wire, and tall fences. There were men walking all around the place with matching uniforms on. The old state blues. Blue pants, blue shirt, belt, white t-shirt, and black boots. This was mandatory with no exceptions. They reminded me of a bunch of zombies just wondering aimlessly. It seemed as if the highlight of their day was the bus pulling into the facility. The bus came to an abrupt stop, and the guards said everyone sit tight until your name is called. That is what we did. Soon they said Teter, Ellsworth. This is where you get off, and where you are staying. I got up and exited the bus. I went inside of Admissions and Discharge where they uncuffed, and unshackled me.

I seen several other inmates while I was waiting to get my blues, my bed roll, and my picture taken. They were actually in a cheerful mood. The only reason I could imagine for this type of behavior is because they get to see new people everyday. They were whistling, and singing along to a song that was on the radio. I felt very upset for this behavior that they were displaying. I just wanted to get out of their, and get to my bunk. However, I still had to go to the clinic to get checked out. Once they were finished with me they told me the cell house and cell number that I would be going to. They put me in H Pod in building four which was a brand new building at the time.

I didn't know it until a day later, but H Pod just so happened to be the segregation unit for the facility. They place you here temporarily until a bunk opens up out in the general population. Once the bunk comes available you get your things together and head for the new cell house. My day came and they sent me to A Pod in building two. I went to the officer station, they gave me a key, and my room number to the cell. I walked into the pod and it was pretty big. Had a TV in the day room, an ice machine, and four tables where the fellas could sit down and play some cards. I went up the stairs, took a right turn, and headed for my door. I put the key in, it popped open and there was my new bunk. At the time it looked rather inviting so I just threw my things in the locker, put my bunk together and crawled up on it and closed my eyes. I was drifting away slowly, that is the last thing that I remember until I woke up.

My Bunkie ended up being an older white man in his fifties. I can not remember his name, but he was a good old dude. He asked me if I had ever been in Ellsworth before, and I said no. He said you'll like it here, this is the Bible belt. I asked him what that meant, and he said Christianity is a truly strong belief out here. People are really different than people other places. I thought that was kind of weird, I never thought about how people are in different places. I come to find out that he was correct. I thought the people were rather understanding for being correction officers. They treated me like I was still a human being, and not a piece of dirt.

We had a good routine, we both worked so we hit the bunk about the same time every night. I would be lying on my bunk and see the glow of a lamp coming up from his bunk. Finally one night I asked him what it is that he spends so much time reading every night and he said The Holy Bible. Then he asked me if I ever heard of it so I just rolled over without answering his question. Why? Because I didn't need to hear that nonsense about how some invisible force can transform my entire life, and deliver me from bondage. Out of nowhere he said that is my exact reaction to the Word as well, I was a man who knew it all. Yet, look at me. I'm an old man in prison, and I will never leave prison. Kid, you have another chance at life, you can still be redeemed , and live out the life that God planned for you if you would just listen to him. After that incident, he never brought it up to me again.

As I became familiar with the yard, and the rest of the prison I began to work out with and older gentleman named Timmy Wayne. We became really good friends, and he told me he had a friend named David that he would like me to meet except that he is in El Dorado lockdown at the present time. I asked him why he wanted me to meet this guy, and all he could say is that he is a really good dude, and that he could teach me a lot. I wondered why he was adamant about me learning things, and I never asked him either. One day we were out on the tennis courts playing pickle ball, and this dude came walking down the sidewalk with this huge smile on his face.

Timmy started hollering at him, and making these crazy loud noises. He said you aren't going to believe this kid, but that is the dude I was talking to you about, that is David. He came up to us and gave Timmy a big hug, and they shook hands. Then Timmy introduced me to him. He just smiled and shook my hand. It was crazy weird for real because I have never had someone be so accepting of me in my entire life. We began to talk a little bit, and we became best friends. He is the best friend I have ever had in my life, and he is still the best friend that I have today. God bless you David. I pray the Lord continues to bless you beyond your understanding, and gives you the chance that you so much deserve.

Come to find out, he got out of lockdown to be a part of the IFI Program; (Initiative, Faith, Interchange). It is a Christ base program that offers many different opportunities to better yourself in life. Dave and I would walk the yard together everyday, and we would always talk about life. What got us their, what we would be doing if we weren't their, and what we are going to do when we get out. I remember it like yesterday. I now know why God placed this man in my life, he knew the gift that I had, and he was able to speak to me in a way no other ever could. The Lord used him to give me the courage that I lacked. However, at the time I didn't know it, I didn't understand.

There were days when we would just walk the yard and he would just quote scripture after scripture to me. Then he would explain what they meant so I could understand them. I would think about them for a few, and like always, I would end up dismissing them altogether I thought. He always told me good things about myself, but I just couldn't believe it, I felt truly unworthy because all of my wrongdoing. Dave and I kicked it for almost two years in Ellsworth, and I learned a great amount from him. This dude has a gang of wisdom along with knowledge to share with other people. Unfortunately, Dave and I ended up getting into some trouble.

I went through many trials and tribulations while at Ellsworth. I got in trouble several different times for dangerous contraband, debt adjustment, gambling, and theft. I would say the most serious trouble that I embarked upon was being involved in racial activity. One morning I was asleep on my bunk when the police opened the door, said my name and told me to get dressed. I complied and they walked me to the unit teams office. When the door opened all I seen was a boat load of hand cuffs. They presented me with this piece of paper, told me to sign it and cuffed me up. They took me, two of my bros, and three black guys to the segregation unit for this racial activity. So we all just sat in the hole until they decided to let us out.

The Lord was working on me back then and I didn't even know it, I understand now. I came to a cross road and decided to join the IFI Program and hang out with Dave and a few of the fellas. I can honestly say that I joined for the wrong reasons. I hadn't been over their for a week and I was already involved in the cigarette business. I didn't know what I was doing. To me I justified it in my head as just trying to get by. It was truly different than general population because the days started out at five in the morning, and you had classes all the way up to eight, nine o'clock at night. I know this by watching the other fellas involved. Myself, I didn't even make it through the orientation process which is thirty days.

I got a job as a cell house porter while in orientation. I was playing cards one morning in G Pod when I seen them escorting Dave to the segregation unit. I didn't know what was going on at the time. Then the officer asked me to take some clothes in the detag cart into the seg unit. At the time I didn't know, but he tricked me. After I got the clothes in the hamper, the officer in the unit asked me if my name was Teter and I said yes. He said to come over here, I complied. He then said give me your ID. I handed him my ID, and asked what this was all about. He said you are being placed in the segregation unit until further notice.

The entire situation ended up being over cigarettes. They were making an example out of me and David. They sent David to Lansing, and they sent me to El Dorado. To this day I believe there was more behind it than that, but that is water under the bridge. Right now at this very point in time I can only say one thing. I thank God for you David, and I thank you brother. You may never know how much you influenced my life in a good way, I will tell you this, I will never stop praying for your release because I know you brother. I know you like the Administration doesn't know you. I know that all you need is that second chance in life, may the Lord continue to bless you beyond your understanding.

The morning I got on the bus in Ellsworth was truly inviting. It was the end of November in the year of 2005. To me this is a beautiful time of year because the transition from summer to winter is in God's hands. The entire landscape is much more colorful, brings joy to my heart. The attitudes of many people are winding down because it's no longer hot outside, a person can just enjoy the fresh air and relax. I was looking forward to this trip to El Dorado because it is quite a drive, and the route is different. You are able to see things you normally wouldn't and that's because most aren't on a department of corrections bus. I was excited just because I hadn't seen a regular citizen for many years, I hadn't seen a vehicle rolling down the highway for a minute, and at the time I just realized that I hadn't even seen a tree, a squirrel, etc. After that thought my mood changed to an abyss of darkness, it reminded me where I was at. This is crazy because the bus ride enabled me to forget that I was a prisoner to the state for a few minutes. The only thing I could think was how I took everything for granted in my life, how they had no meaning to me.

The bus pulled into the joint at El Dog. We all sat patiently until we made it thru the check point. The doors came open and they began to take roll call. My name was hollered and I came forward. There was three black suits waiting for me and they escorted me into A&D. They unshackled and uncuffed me. Put me thru the entire process, gave me a bed roll and sent me on my way. I went to a place called U-Dorm. This is an open dorm where you can move around and do what you please as long as you aren't in violation of the rules. I got my bunk area straightened out and decided to lay down and soak it all in. I woke up after count and decided to walk around and get familiar with the place that was now my temporary home. I ran across a few fellas that I had done time with before.

Went to chow that night, came back to the dorm and right before yard a dude came up to me and asked me if my name was Michael Teter, I said yes. He asked me if I knew this dude, I said yes. He said he wants you to meet him in the bathroom at yard to finish some business that was left in Ellsworth. I said cool, tell him I will be their. So when they called yard, I went to the gym bathroom to fight this dude. I said to myself, wow! Nice way to start the first day off at a new joint. So I decided I had to put down a demonstration, I mean what is another fight. You do ten years in the joint you are going to have to fight, but this time was different. I really didn't anticipate this barbaric opportunity like before, I wasn't feeding off of the negativity. All I could do is ask myself what the world is wrong with you kid? I had been in so many fights with the police and beaten up, so many fights with other convicts and now my heart is telling me something different.

I was tripping or something, now wasn't the time to become a man with feelings of this sort. God was in my corner for real, I didn't know it, and I didn't understand it at the time but I do now. I went to that bathroom that night and dude decided that it wasn't necessary after all. For the first time in my life I felt relief when it comes to a situation like this. Besides, we were friends at one time. It's like this, I can compare this situation symbolically to the devil wanting the power of God. We were all bros, this dude decided that his way was better so in his own selfish ways he started strife and division among us. He was wrong, unlike the devil, he finally realized it. After that we shook hands and went our own separate ways, we didn't hang out or anything like that. We talked in the passing of one another, and one time we ended up in the hole right next to each other. I know it happened for a reason, we had the opportunity to talk a little deeper about things which was a blessing. I woke up in the hole one day and he was gone.

I landed a job in the laundry doing all the reds, and bed rolls from RDU. This was a cool job because it was at late night when everyone else is in bed. I worked with a couple of dudes that became dear friends, and today they still are. I call one of them no fuss Russ, his favorite thing to say is love, peace, and chicken grease. I never heard anything like it. The other fella, his name is Mark, we were bunkies for quite awhile. I believe he lives in New York right now doing very well. We did a lot of stuff together, eat, smoke, and get into trouble. It was crazy, but some of the greatest memories that I have. Mark got out in 2005. One day I was running on the yard in Lansing back in the beginning of 2009 and he pops up on the track. He was back doing a parole violation. Haven't seen nor heard from him since. Hope you are doing well Mark. God bless you brother.

The laundry gig didn't last very long. I ended up getting several class one write ups and going to the hole for several months. I had a long time to think about things. I would just lay on my bunk wondering what my family was doing and how they were getting along. I continued to ask myself why must I do the same things over and over and always end up in segregation. As some of you may know El Dorado is known for death row and long term segregation. I came to know many men in this unit that have been down their since the 90's. That gave me inspiration for real. I say this because when men are only down their for a couple of years and you know some have been in the hole for over a decade, somehow you know in your heart you will make it.

Things were really beginning to look up for me when I landed a porter job in U-dorm where all of the minimum wage workers lived. I made a pretty good living in their. I had several partners as well. A few of the fellas went to bat for me and got me hired at a place known as Century. I couldn't believe it. It wasn't the next week that as I was about to begin to work I was lying on my bunk when the police brought me a box. I said what is this for. He said you are going to Lansing tomorrow morning, you have minimum custody so you have to go. Man I was disgruntled for real. I was about to make some money and once again it was yanked out from under me like it was never their. I asked myself, is this ever going to end.

I got up and packed all of my belongings and said my goodbyes. I really didn't want to leave because I had many good friends their. I have to say this, Michael Greer, God bless you kid. I haven't forgot about you brother. I know how you must feel right now, but I am only human and those words did not come out right bro. I pray everyday that you will forgive me for what I said and how I put it. God bless you and your family brother.

The bus rolled up to Lansing on a cold November night back in 2006. I believe it was a couple days before Thanksgiving. We went into A&D and went through the old drill. They gave us our clothes and told us where we were going. I remember those walls when we pulled up in front of the place. I was truly in awe. I just wanted to see what was back their. I heard of Lansing my entire life yet I could never imagine it. It brought one thing to mind. Even though I am only a human being, I could see that wall in my heart metaphorically speaking. The wall that separates me and everyone behind it from true freedom, peace, and love. That would be myself. The only thing that stands in our way is self. I lived many years believing that I am not worthy of any type of goodness that is offered in life. However, that is so far from the truth friends. It is only when we give our life will we find the true meaning of life.

At first it didn't make any sense to me so I had to pray about it and the Lord revealed it to me. We know, For God so loved the world that he gave his only Son, so that everyone who believes in Him will not perish but have eternal life. **John 3:16 NLT.** Sense God created us in his own image, and we are to lead by example as Jesus did by being the perfect sacrifice for all before, now, and after, then it only conveys the message that when we to give our life by entrusting it to God will we find what life is truly about.

It was getting late and all I really wanted to do was just lay down. For some reason I just wanted this to be over with. My patients were growing truly short and though CO at A&D was truly admitting he. He tried to put me in a blue jump suit required to transport from the max to the minimum. That was two sizes too small for me. I said to myself, " If this man doesn't give me a different outfit I probably wont be going to the minimum tonight." He complied to my wishes. So I grabbed my things and got on the little white bus. There were approximately five gentlemen heading the same direction that I was.

I found it rather funny. That I was stuffed in this bus with a ton of property and the transporting officer couldn't even speak English. The giant overhead door came open and he backed out into the parking lot. Remember, It's November which means ice and snow on the ground. So while driving you would think that we would take precaution to the weather conditions. As we pulled out onto the road and began our journey to the hill I could see ahead of me several sharp curves and twists in the road. The next thing I know the ass end of this van slid right out from underneath us and the

Asian guy driving the van began to panic while screaming things I couldn't even begin to understand.

I know to this day that that van was in gods hands. I don't know how he did it but some how he regained control over the van. I know it sounds crazy. Being only a quarter mile away. I thought we were going to die on that bus that night. I thank god to this day that he gave the CO that ability to overcome what I thought for sure was a tragedy about to happen. As we came out of it he began to utter words in a very soft manner. Although I couldn't understand what he was saying I believe he was thanking god. I say this because I saw him lean forward and look up into the sky as he was saying those words. About five minutes passed and we were pulling up into the minimum in one piece and happy to be alive.

We all got out of the van and grabbed our property. We went to the clinic and got all our bed rolls and headed for the dorm. They put me in a place called the S dorm. It was the most run down dorm on the hill and probably had the most knuckle heads in it. I just figured that's why I was there. I went up stairs found my bunk and began to make it. I introduced myself to my Bunkie and told him I would be going to sleep now because I've had a long day on the bus. His name was Fletcher.

The next morning he woke me up and offered me some hot coffee and a package of pop tarts. I accepted the invitation and we had a really good conversation. He worked up in the kitchen and asked me if I would like to have a job up there. I told him, " yeah that would be cool." So he said that when he went to work that he would talk to his supervisor and see if she would hire me. She said that I could come in and talk to her and she would make a decision then. So the next morning I got a pass from the CO and went up to the chow hall to talk to this lady. She ended up giving me a job on the serving line. It turned out to be pretty beneficial for my schedule because I only worked for three hours a day. I got to eat anything I wanted but I was partial to fruits, vegetables, and tuna fish.

A few days passed and I was out in the weight pit doing some dead lifts when I heard a voice say,"Teter?" I said,"yeah." He said,"Michael Teter? From Garnett?" I said,"yeah. What's up?" He said," Its me. Jason. From Ottawa." I was like," What? What are you doing in here?" He came over and started talking to me which gave us the opportunity to catch up on all the time we hadn't seen each other. He said that he was working in the canteen and living over in R dorm. Which is really laid back. He asked me where I lived and I said S dorm. He said if you want to move over to R Dorm I can probably help you get moved over there. As soon as a bunk came open in his cube I moved over there and we began to kick it. It was like we were back home again, I can now say that it was a blessing.

After I moved over with Jason I began to get more comfortable and slowly got involved in some things that I probably shouldn't have. I started selling contraband and I made enough money doing that to get me a few perks. The main reason I wanted a cell phone was truly an act of desperation. I hadn't seen nor heard from any of my family for years and I just felt the need to talk to my mother. It wasn't the greatest decision that I made but it served the purpose. I spoke with my mother a couple of times and found no encouragement in the conversations that we had. At the time I didn't know all the details to what was going on out here. I guess the word got out that I had a cell phone and the police were eager to find it.

I woke up one beautiful morning in May to go to the weight pit and do the work out with my friend Michael. When out of no where. Came five black suites with a dog. I just figured they were going to look for some drugs or something. So I kept on walking. As I passed them they yelled hey you come here. My name is not hey you. So I kept on walking. They yelled hey you again. Still I kept on walking. Unfortunately they yelled Teter stop. When I heard my name hit my hears I took off at a dead run. And the race was on. I smashed these dudes. The first dorm I came into I ran into the bathroom and kicked the last stall door open. There was someone in there. I said my bad bro and went to the next one which was open. I immediately flushed the stool. Pulled the sock out of my pants and flushed what was inside. It all went down except the charger, just a bit to small. I grabbed it and threw it in the trash.

I pulled my sweat shirt off because it had my name on the back of it and threw it over the partition hoping they wouldn't recognize me and just keep on searching. Boy was I wrong. As soon as they saw me. They snatched me up. Threw me on the ground and cuffed me up. They asked me what I flushed and I said I don't know what you're talking about. They said yeah whatever. They said you will be going to jail pending investigation. I said cool. You ready? They walked me to the little white van and transported me back to the walls. As we were driving I could see those enormous walls from the distance. I thought wow! Finally I get to see what the Devils front porch looks like from the inside. I was excited. I know it sounds odd but I couldn't wait to get out of segregation and I wasn't even there yet.

I just recently realized something after doing all these years in prison and that realization is that I was only visitor during this long journey. I never succumbed to what prison truly is to many people. I did on the outside exterior, but not on the inside. I looked at it as an opportunity to help others overcome their feeling of no hope. Yet I had none. All I had was a void inside my heart that I attempted to fill by using anything I could get my hands on no matter what the cost. Even though I felt that way I couldn't handle seeing another man striving to fill the existing void in their heart. I guess you could say at the time my hypocrisy was as deep as the ocean. I would tell one of my friends that you don't need to do that stuff. You're getting out soon. Get out there and love someone. Don't let this be the end of the road. Nine times out of ten they would reply what about you man? What about you? I would just be like Bro not only do I not deserve it I'm not worthy of any goodness. This is where I shall remain until they decide to let me go. That is how I justified it. At this point in time I just settled. I guess you could call it the easy way out.

But what I didn't realize at this point in time was that you only get what you give. I can honestly say that I gave a lot. However, I could not accept anything that someone would offer or would like to do for me. That's just the way it was and at the time I was cool with that. As long as I was on empty I didn't have to worry about any of that. I just call it the road to self destruction. Next thing I know I'm getting off the van and being escorted to C cell house. Which is known as the segregation unit in Lancing. We walked in the door. They dressed me out. Gave me a bedroll and threw me in my cell.

Once again I managed to screw up, as usual. I made it to minimum camp where I had it made. However, I took all the freedom for granted. I'm sitting on my bunk and only one question comes to my mind. Michael, why do you always have to do everything the hard way? It continued to cross my mind. Over, and over as I paced the floor in that tiny cell. I didn't know what to do. My heart was crying out. But I just couldn't speak the words. Only because I didn't want to seem weak. Insanity, Misery, and for what? To maintain a reputation that you really don't even know if it exists. Honestly in my heart I just wanted to succumb to what I know now as the Holy spirit. Unfortunately my flesh overcame the spirit side of me. I just took a deep breath and said I can do this. I've done it many other times so I know ill get through it.

As the hours passed by I just wanted to take a nap. But that's hard to do when your mind just wont stop racing. So you just lay there until you're just extremely exhausted and you just cant stay awake any longer. I woke up to a young man saying Teter Teter you need to sign this paper. I looked up at him and said what is it for? He said it is your disciplinary report for running from the black suits at the minimum. Sign it, take a copy. Be ready to go to court on the above date. I said alright thank you. Well, I had something to look forward to once again. My fate was in their hands, as usual.

The days were very long and the nights were even longer. I had nothing in my cell to keep me occupied. I had no books, I had no writing supplies, I had nothing. Just a bedroll. Next thing you know. I started singing parts of songs that I knew just to get through the day. I really didn't have anything to look forward to. The meals were the same thing over and over. About a week had passed and I finally got some paper and a pen and I was able to write a couple letters and jot a few ideas down.

One day out of no where the guy next to me said is your name Teter. I said yea why? He said I have a boy named Tommy that had mentioned the name Teter to me before. I said really? What's his last name? He said Ferris. I said really I know Tommy Ferris. He was one of my cellies while I was in Ellsworth back in 2003. He said yea my boy is following his old mans footsteps. I said well how's Tommy doing? He said he's doing pretty well. He's living up in Topeka and has a little girlfriend. He said I hope that she can keep him out of trouble. I said that's good. Cuz I know Tommy's a pretty good kid and has a lot of potential. He said that's ironic. My boy said the same thing about you. I said really? He said yea. He told me that you don't even seem like you should be in prison. I really didn't know what to say to that. And he said you're a good man and I don't even know you. But I know just from what I've heard about you. I don't think anyone has ever told me anything so touching, me a good man. That is one thing I haven't heard much of.

Me and Ferris became pretty good friends and we lived next to one another for about a month before he went back out to the minimum. I'll give the old man this. He sure gave me a lot to think about. The greatest thing I remember him saying to me is you know mike. There is a god and he is real. I never knew why he said that to me until months later. You see this man was conveying a message to me from god himself. I say this because I now know that god uses people that believe in him. I never saw this man again. But I am truly grateful for the kind words that he spoke to me. I mean think about it. I'm sitting in the hole in Lansing penitentiary. A truly dark place. And the man next to me spoke of God. Who would have ever thought that that word would even be uttered in such a place. I remember the day he left like it was yesterday. He walked past my cell with the police behind him and he stopped momentarily and all he did was point upward. At the time I didn't even know what he was saying. But I know now. This is just more evidence that the light will snuff out the darkness. Praise God!

The day came, they said Teter turn around and back up to the bean hole and place your hands behind your back. I did as they said. They put handcuffs on me. Then they told me to step away from the door. And the door came open. They escorted me to the hearing room over my disciplinary report. I sat down. While she asked me a serious question. She said Mr. Teter do you understand the consequences behind the d.r. in question. I said yes. She said do you understand that if found guilty you can remain in the hole until the administration decides to let you out. I said yes I do. She said how do you plea to the charge of avoiding an officer? I said not guilty. She said answer one question for me. I said what might that question be? Why did you run from the black suits? I said that I had to go to the bathroom really bad. She actually started laughing and said are you serious? And I said yes mam I was having a really bad day. She said that is the most ridiculous answer I think I've ever gotten from anyone who has ever ran from the police in here. Therefore I find you guilty as charged and you shall remain in special management until further notice.

I was in awe. I couldn't believe this lady didn't believe me. My heart sunk. Only god knows how long I would remain in this hole. I was just like forget it. I just started acting a fool. Talking trash to the police. Throwing things out on the run. Talking bad to other inmates, etc. Just like all the other fellas around me. I did this for like a week maybe. It got old quick. I told myself this isn't you. Why are you doing this. It makes no sense. I need to find something constructive to do. I decided to put a form 9 into mental health and ask them for some cross word puzzles and stuff. The next day the unit team came to my door and said here's your cross word puzzles Mr. Teter enjoy them. I said thank you. Man these puzzles really exercised my mind. I figured they would be easy but they were extremely time consuming. It was a blessing for real. I spent hours working on these things and I wouldn't stop until I had them all completed.

One day I decided to write mental health about the cross word puzzles and ask them if they had something a little less challenging. I received my response one day and on it said we give out these puzzles based on the information we have about you. I was lost. I didn't understand what they were talking about. There response was a new stack of puzzles. I glanced over them real quick and said what are they trying to do to me. The puzzles were more complex than the ones I had before. I didn't understand what they were doing until a later date. One day one of the therapists was making his rounds in the segregation room and when he stopped at my cell I asked him about the cross word puzzles. He said that the whole idea behind the puzzles were designed to make us think. To occupy our minds while we are struggling. I said oh I see. The only thing else I could say was thank you. I must admit my time went by better when I had the puzzles as compared to when I didn't.

Its amazing what a small book can do while confined to a tiny cell. You already have nothing and at the same time your heart is yeaning for something. Suddenly a crossword puzzle is introduced to the equation and hope is rediscovered. In the back of your mind you're thinking maybe, just maybe there is a reason for all of this adversity and you are doing everything you can to hold on. That question continued to occupy my time, I couldn't think of anything else. Is there hope for me, is there any reason not to give these people havoc. They are keeping me from my freedom. One day I finally realized that these people were just doing their jobs, they are there to help us if we make the correct choice. Sad to say, but if we don't make the correct choice they will discipline us accordingly. I thank God for the day he brought understanding to my heart concerning authority figures.

I found a routine to get through my days which made them more bearable. Finally that day came when the police showed up in front of my cell and said Mr. Teter pack your things, you are going to D cell house. I was on it, I was ready for something different in my life other than the hole. I couldn't wait to get out and move around even though it was behind some gigantic walls. I could actually stretch my legs and jump around if I wanted to. This is the cell house where it all happened friends. I thank God for placing me in that cell house. I walked in the door and approached the encased glass window. The cop said can I help you and I said Teter. He said cell 206, second run. I walked in and went up the stairs, took a right and wouldn't you know it. The cell was right there only a couple cells from the lock box. The police stand there all of the time. I was thinking man, couldn't you move me farther down the run. You see, I was already thinking about all of the things I was going to get off that I'm not suppose to. Imagine that!

I had no clue where my life was going. I just knew that I went from a small cell to another cell. I knew several people in Lansing at the time so I wasn't to shook. When I walked on the run in D cell house I felt all eyes on me. They popped my cell door and I asked the officer on duty if I could clean my cell. He said I could just not to take all day. I really appreciated the cooperation because moving right into a cell after someone else and not being able to clean it just isn't cool. I took my time sweeping it, mopping it, and wiping everything down real well. After I got that done I was able to put my bunk together and put everything away. I put every thing away and told the officer that I was finished and he told me to lock down. I went into my new house and layed on my bunk just soaking in the new seen that I was just dropped in. There wasn't anyone in the cells next to me so I wondered who my neighbors were and when they would be in. I decided to read some of my book to help the time pass quicker. I was full of anticipation, I was eager to locate a way of escape because it had been awhile since I had done anything being in the hole all that time.

The yard was called in and a young man came up in front of my cell. I thought how crazy is this to myself. They put me right next door to a good friend of mine. With him being by my side I knew I would be in the game before the day was over with. We spent quite a while on the hill together getting into everything we possibly could. We had a good time, that's what we call it in their. Him and I would get up early every morning because I was a porter and we would go out on the balcony and smoke a stick of herb(marijuana). We called it getting our head right and getting ready for the rest of the day. He would hang out in my dorm and then later on we would cook something to eat and just chill. We would talk about our life, our families, and our dreams. That's the thing, we would just talk. We would never take action, it's almost like we expect someone else to do it for us. I know that sounds crazy, but it is true. I haven't met one man in prison that didn't have a special gift. They just lack the guidance and direction, I know from experience.

When my bro saw me he had a big smile on his face. First thing he did was ask me if I needed anything. I said no I'm cool. This kid has a heart of gold, he always made sure that I didn't go without and he didn't have to. He stood in front of my cell for about ten, fifteen minutes while the showers were running filling me in on the details about where we now are. I said bro, where's the herb? He said don't even trip, I will holler at you soon as I get into my cell. I told him that I have three hundred cash and we should just get a big sack and stay lit for as long as we can. He just started laughing. He said trying to make up for the hole time aren't you, I said but of course, any other way would just be uncivilized. He said let me talk to someone and see what I can do. I was like cool.

He locked down and not ten minutes had passed when he said hey Tet, I said what's up kid? Come to the bars. I went to the bars and he had his mirror out on the run so I grabbed mine. Put your hand out here. I put my hand out there and he placed a piece of paper in it. I pulled it in, opened it and it was a nice chunk of herb. I broke it up, rolled it, made a one hitter, got everything ready and took it straight to the head. Man it felt good. Just like old times. I didn't realize how close it was to lunch, wasn't twenty minutes after I got my head right the doors popped open. I went out on the run and waited for my neighbor. We were laughing and carrying on enjoying the escape from reality. On the way to the chow hall I seen several fellas I was cool with that chatted me up saying it was good to see me and all this jazzy stuff. After we got our food we sat down at the table and he told me the deal was done. I was to give him the money and he could hook up a fat sack and we could smoke for days. That sounded like a plan to me. Later that day I gave him the money and a gut dropped off a fat sack and we were in hog heaven, literally. I rolled up some fat hooters and we partied like we were on the bricks. I looked out for a few other fellas that I had done time with that were in the cell house with us.

During this little escapade I kept noticing this Mexican dude around my area. He was an older gentleman. I noticed him because it seemed like he wanted me to. The way he kept looking at me was quite puzzling. I don't recall anytime another person looked at me this way. I was heading back to my cell one day after skating over to the other side of the cell house to talk to one of my bros. I seen the fella up ahead of me. At first I didn't know what to think or do. So I just put my head up and continued my journey. As I walked by him I felt him looking at me even after I passed him. Something told me to stop, turn around and see what's up. I did this and he was at a stand still. I said what's up man, I have noticed you keep looking at me in a weird way. Do you have a problem with me or something? He said no brother, I need to tell you something. I said what's up? He walked up to me, looked me straight in the eyes and said I see God in you brother. He turned right around and went about his business. I was dumbfounded. I didn't know what this meant. I see God in you. How was I suppose to react to that.? No man has ever uttered those words to me before. I had no clue what that meant. God, who is he? Why would he be in me?

I lockdown and I go sit on my bunk. What the old man said to me keeps running through my head. Why would he tell me such nonsense? I have heard of this God before but don't know anything about him. Now I thought to myself, if you have something in you wouldn't you want to know about it? I felt in my heart that I did. However, I didn't know how to go about this situation. I do know this, in prison God isn't very popular. That is one fact I did know, but I didn't know why. I also knew one other thing at this time. I need to get out of this cell and get into another one away from the police station. I put in a form 9 to the unit team and several days later I got to move up to the third run almost to the end. I was happy that they moved me because it brought new opportunity to my life, just not in a good way. I knew several of the fellas up here and have done a lot of time with them. The big plus is that the police don't travel this run as much as the others. That is a good thing.

I was really liking my situation at that time. I was kickin it with the fellas, not a worry in the world. I spent my days drawing cards, writing letters, smoking dope, and drinking hooch. When I didn't have any of these things I would just be depressed and lay around. I couldn't escape from the reality of being in a cage. Many succumb to it but for some unknown reason I didn't. For a long time I didn't know the answer to the mystery. It was like something deep down inside of this dark abyss was trying to see the light. It knew, but I didn't. The yearning kept getting bigger and bigger, honestly it was killing me inside. I just wanted all of this pain and suffering to be over with, however, I didn't know where to begin. So I did what I thought was the most logical, I began to ask questions. I would talk to older gentlemen that had already done many years in the prison. They would have to know what I was talking about, surely they have been through the same experience as I was going through at the time.

Because I was charged with rape and aggravated kidnapping I was required to go through treatment. Now this is complex my friends. Because I was living in the dark I believed all the things all other prisoners were saying about this treatment group. You can not imagine some of the things I heard about this. Can you fathom the idea of being in prison and then some people trying to get it through your thick skull that they are there to help you. That they want to see you succeed. I'm no different than anyone else, I thought they were just filling my head full of nonsense. I truly thought that they were looking for a reason to keep me inside those walls for the rest of my life.

While I was in prison a few of my family members wrote me and told me that my dad was sick, but they never went into any detail about it. Honestly, the last time I saw him he looked pretty good. The last thing I remember doing with him is playing a game of cards that I learned how to play the first time I was in prison. I will never forget that. My mom would write and she would say your dad is a little sick, but he should be alright. I wasn't trippin because I kind of lost touch of reality. It's almost like you have to let everything go inside the walls so you can be on top of your game. You have to stay on your toes. It's all about survival of the fittest.

One day all of reality set in like never before. I got up that morning and went to my treatment class just like every other day. I have to be honest with you. When I first started this it was my goal to give them nothing but chaos. I was being hard headed and a smart ass every chance I got. Why? Because I knew in my heart that they really didn't have no interest what so ever to help me. Maybe at the time I just didn't want to help myself. It's difficult to think that any type of goodness exists in so much darkness. Group was over and it was time to go back to my cell and wait for lunch.

I walked into the cell house and the police asked me why I wasn't in the visitation room. I thought ok, so you have jokes do ya. I said I don't get any visits you must be mistaking. He said no, you have a visit so you need to go up their. I said why are you just telling me now. They had no answer. Usually if you get a visit and you are not in the cell house it is the officers duty to call the place where you are and let you know. Make a long story short, that didn't happen. I was truly upset for real and had a few choice words for the officer responsible for the situation.

I went up to the visitation room. I gave the officer my pass and he let me in. I told them my name and they said ok. I was pretty excited because I had only seen my mother twice in the last eight years and the rest of my family, none. I looked around the room and saw no one that I recognize. I looked at the officer and asked if he had the right Teter because there were two other fellas in Lansing with almost the same spelling of the last name as mine. He read the number and it was mine. He said the man here to see me is over there in the wheel chair. I looked while standing there and had no recollection of who it was. I began to walk over there and I saw the tattoos on his arm. My heart sunk, I thought the last time I saw him we were playing cards and having a good time. I wanted to turn around and leave. I was already in enough pain.

I went over there and sat down next to him, I was speechless. There was a man with him and he introduced himself as Matthew. He was the hospice care giver who brought my dad to see me. He informed me of the situation. He said your dad wanted to come see you Michael, your mother and your sister came as well but the prison would not let them in. The only thing I could say is what is going on here. What has happened to him? Matthew told me that he contracted Lou Gehrig's Disease. He went on to explain to me that it is a rare condition and the doctors don't know much about it. He said that there is nothing they can do except make him comfortable as possible until the time comes.

I couldn't believe I was setting here listening to all of this. I mean I knew he was sick, but I had no idea that it was like this. I turned to talk to my dad and Matthew told me that he can't speak. He has lost everything that makes it possible. He said he can understand everything you say, he just can't respond to anything. I didn't know what to say or to do. I just started talking to him because somehow I knew it was going to be the last time I was to see or talk to him. Right before they called the visit I seen this look in his eyes. It was compelling, almost like he was trying to tell me something. I leaned in to give him a hug and my left ear was by his mouth. His last words as he whispered to me was, boy, I hope you are saved some day. I had no idea what that meant. I leaned up and kissed him for the last time on the forehead. Today, I know it was the Holy Spirit. The Lord says may the Holy Spirit draw you closer, and that is what it did.

Matthew got up and began to wheel him away. I just said to myself, I love you dad. That was the day my entire life changed. Who would of ever guessed. I sat there for a few minutes before the co came and got me so I could go back to my cell house. I believe he did that out of respect, just to give me some time to get my bearings back. I went back to my cell house and the officer who neglected to call treatment and let me know that I had a visit tried to talk to me. I said dude, they only sat up there for thirty minutes wondering where I was at and I only got to see my dad who is dying for twenty minutes, no big deal. Then I went to my cell. I stood there for about ten minutes before they opened my door just in awe. I couldn't make up my mind if this was really happening or not. That's what happens when you are doing time. It's like life just stops for you and everything on the outside is still the same as the day you walked into the joint.

My cell door finally popped open and I entered. I sat down on my bunk and closed my eyes. The next thing I know I was going to the floor where I ended up on my knees. I put my elbows on the bunk, lowered my head, and clasped my hands together. I said God, if you are there show me. Help me, I'm tired of all of this pain and suffering. I'm tired of being something I'm not. I just want to be me, I no longer want to pretend. I said God, if you are there please forgive me for all of the wrong things I've done in my life and help me be a better man. I said I can not do this on my own, please help me. I just told him how I felt on the inside, I just gave it all to him. When I got up I felt this calm inside of me, never felt anything like it before. I felt anew, I felt like I had a purpose in this life after all and I never turned back.

Everything happens for a reason, I do know this, and it is for God's glory. My first question was what does it mean to be saved? I started asking questions about it and the best advice I got from a man was to pray about it. The first chance I got after lockdown I got on my knees and asked the Lord to reveal what to be saved means. It was the next day that a fella brought a Bible by my cell and I began to read it. The Bible that he gave me is called the Life Recovery Bible, New Living Translation. It is the most distributed Bible today and I thank God that he brought it my way. I began to read it and I couldn't put it down. I couldn't believe all of the things that it said. It's all about truth, wisdom, love, etc. I have never seen nor heard of any of this stuff in this way. I found it exciting because I had no idea that anything like this existed in life. I felt the sweet essence of hope yearning inside of me once again like never before.

I came in from yellow yard one afternoon after a good workout. Went and grabbed all of my shower gear, took a shower and went back to my cell. I took care of everything and laid down on my bunk waiting for count to clear. The craziest thing happened. During count I seen a group of black suits walk into the cell house. Then the police said Teter, when count clears we need you to come down here. I thought wow! I'm going back to segregation once again. After count, the door popped open which I thought was weird because if you are going to jail they would meet you right at the door.

I stepped out onto the run and I just felt that something was wrong. I went towards the office and when I came around the corner I saw the Chaplain of the prison. I thought this can not be good. When this dude comes to visit you it's usually because some one has passed away. He said will you step into the Unit Team's office with me. I did. He closed the door, we sat down. He said I don't know how to say this but I must tell you. You father passed away on September 15th. I was quiet. I thought to myself how can this be, it is September 22nd, and you are just now telling me. I guess this is the price you pay for being in prison even when it comes to death. He went on to further explain that the message got lost in the mix and that he apologizes for the delay. I mean what could I say or do about it besides take it for what it is. The answer is nothing. To this day I don't believe that it was on purpose, the administration has a great amount of inmates to handle and not enough staff to accomplish that task.

Then and there I knew why the black suits were in the house. I believe it is procedure in times like this because in the past I have seen some prisoners just absolutely lose it. So they take them to segregation where they can be monitored closely, also so they will not harm themselves or others. Everyone acts differently in situations like this and it is there job to make sure everyone is safe. The Chaplain told me that if there is anything he can do for me to just let him know. I told him I was good, not to worry about me. I went back to my cell and one of the co's working, Mr. Bausch, a young man told me that he was sorry for my loss. I just said thank you. I went back to my cell, got on my knees and said Lord this is it. I now know what it means to be saved, and I know you used my dad for a great reason. What is it, I have no idea at this time but I hope and pray to find out one day. I thank God for using my dad that day out in the visitation room. It was his perfect timing, no one else could of done it. I do know this, I made a promise that I intend to keep.

I do know this from experience my friends, I denounced God all of my life. I just couldn't fathom the idea of believing in something that I can't see with my own eyes. Well, once again I was wrong. I searched for something different in my life the entire time I was in prison and nothing brought me peace. The only thing that was left was the one thing that claims it will bring you the peace and joy that your heart desires. How ironic, the one thing, God. He did it and at the perfect time, and I am so thankful for that. He saved my life. It doesn't matter what you have done in your life. He is all forgiving and this is the truth. No man can do that, no woman can do that, only God. His love is unconditional for all of those who believe in them, hallelujah!

God took off in my life quickly. He opened doors and gave me opportunities right out the gate. Many people knew my dad had passed and they just couldn't believe how I was handling the situation so well. Some even had the courage to ask me and the only thing I could tell them is that God has given me peace about it, and all things. I remember the first time I ever spoke his name out loud to another individual in prison. I thought to myself did I just say that to him. I did, and when I did it there was no hesitation. I noticed this immediately. The look that he had on his face was puzzling, I don't think he realized what I just said or he just couldn't believe that I said it was God. That is when I decided that God is doing this for a reason. I mean I was lost and empty, I had no hope whatsoever. Then this God comes along and gives me life for what it truly is, indeed, I'm going to speak about it. The feeling that he has given me on the inside is something that we all should experience, it is like nothing this world has to offer. Nothing in this world can compare to it in anyway shape, or form. That's how great it is. True freedom! Because God gave it to me, I just want to give it to everyone else I come in contact with so they to can enjoy what life truly is.

I will not lie about the situation, early on there were times when I thought maybe this isn't real and I almost turned my back on God. Even after we give our life to the Lord doesn't mean that we will not go through trials and tribulations. The important thing to know is what God has done for us. Probably the most popular Scripture ever quoted. **John 3:16 NLT**-For God so loved the world that he gave his only Son, so that everyone who believes in him will not perish but have eternal life. NLT. This is the truth my friends, it means exactly what it says. Think about it, humanly speaking our child is the most precious thing in our life. God didn't even spare his only son hoping you will benefit from it. That's how great his love is for all of those who believe in him. He already gave you the greatest gift in life, so there is nothing else you could possibly ask for that he will not give you. That is why you should know that he will give whatever you ask for in his time, not yours.

I thank God to this day for what he has done in my life. He has been so good to me. He gave me peace at the right time. I know that if I didn't have the Lord during the time my pops passed away

I would of fell apart. That's why it is important to know that as a believer we are never alone, he is always with us. Anytime I felt down and out I would get on my knees and just talk to him and tell him what I need in my life. I began to see all of this come real, I didn't know what to think about it. I would set around and question myself to the fullest. My mind was always spinning looking for a reason not to believe this. I believe the Lord knew this as well, for he knows all things.

I created this thirst as time went by. As my prayers kept coming true the more excited I became. I couldn't put the Good book down for the life of me. When I wasn't in the chow hall or on the yard working out my face would be in the book. I remember for several years I had this Christian lady writing me faithfully two, three times a week. She would send me letters with Scripture in it telling me that God loves me and that he wants to help me in the fullest. I just thought whatever lady, why are you wasting your time with me. I told a couple of my friends about this situation and they gave me a few ideas. I began to ask her for money and she had no problem sending it to me. I would make all kinds of stories up to get money from her. I would spend the money on my own selfish desires. This lady is still a good friend of mine and she still stands by my side. As the Lord convicted my heart I wanted to tell her the truth. So one day I sat down and composed a letter to her and put it all down on paper.

I came clean for the first time in my life. I know this was a good woman and she didn't deserve this type of treatment from me or anyone else. After I got finished I put the letter on my bunk, got down on my knees and asked the Lord to do what he does. I waited patiently for a response with great anticipation. I did this because I was about to see how great this God truly is. One day I'm sitting on my bunk during count time and the police walked in front of my cell and said Teter. I got up and he handed me a letter. It was a letter from this woman so I opened it up and began to read it. There it was in black and white, I forgive you Michael. I felt tears welling up in my eyes. I couldn't believe it friends, she forgave me and I am sharing this with you because God used her in a great way to show me how unconditional his love is for his children. Today I am so grateful for God's grace and his mercy. This situation helped me more than I understand.

I began to experience the healing in my heart for the first time in my life. I was struggling in this therapy because I didn't want to believe that they wanted to help me. So one night I was sitting in my cell thinking about this situation. I went to the Lord in earnest prayer and asked him what I should do. I did this because I knew he wouldn't lead me astray. He said Michael, take everything I have revealed to you and apply it to your therapy and you will be in awe. At first I was like are you serious, but he gave me the courage I needed to do just that. It was kind of crazy at first because when I started using the Lord's name in group people looked at me weird. I was like well, look at me anyway you want because no person could ever do for me what the love of Jesus Christ has did in my life. I know the truth and I will stand on it is the attitude I had and the attitude I still have. I mean he has been around since the beginning and he is still here today, and he is still saving lives. I know that he is the same yesterday, today, and forever. Besides, many other people speak on what something has done in their life so I shall do the same. I will ask if I can, I have no intention on offending anyone with what I believe in, that is just how loving God is. However, some people have different opinions and that's cool, that is their right.

As time went by in this group therapy I began to realize that I wasn't all alone after all. This is one of the greatest revelations that God revealed to me during my prison sentence. I soon became determined not only to help myself but to help many other men who were struggling as well. I soon learned that everything in life has a balance. There is two sides to everything. Since I was a young child I came to believe that only bad existed and I carried that into my adult hood. It was an awesome day when I seen that if there is bad, there must be good. That is what gave me the ability to go with it, the fact that I hit Rock Bottom. I was desperate and I wanted so bad to believe that love existed. I thank God to this day because it does exist and it is awesome.

It wasn't long before I realized that yes there is many good therapists out there in the world trying to help other people and that is admirable. On the other hand, I found out that the greatest Counselor is Father God, no human can compare to his wisdom. I paid close attention to what was going on. I would listen to what they had to say and I would compare it to what God has written in the good book. If it was in line I would put it in my tool box, if it didn't, I would discard it completely. Then I began to use God's promises to all of his children and implement them and it was a great success. **John 8:32 NLT**-And you will know the truth, and the truth will set you free. It's that simple my friends. I got everything out of my heart for the first time in my life, I was free and it felt so good. NLT.

It's nice to feel free, you do not have to remember anything you said. There is no conflict. It is what it is, you are no longer struggling to be who you are. Finally you find yourself and you don't care what anyone thinks about who you are. The greatest thing you realize is that it is only God who matters because everything you have came from him. I just put it like this, you can love it or leave it. If you no longer want to be my friend because I found the Lord, well, it's your loss not mine because I am now full of unspeakable joy. I know in my heart that my Lord has given me everything that I have to this day. No man, nor woman is capable of doing what God can do in a person's life. Trust me, living in love is so much better than living in misery.

I was lost for thirty five years and the devil had nothing good for me. The only thing he did for me is make sure that I lived in misery. It's a choice that we all make, no one can do it for us. I know not everyone has been to prison but God is not very popular in their. For those of you who don't know, Lansing is known as the Devil's front porch. It's almost like you are sent their to be tested to see where your heart is going to lie for eternity. There are several types of influence in the joint, if you decide to take a positive route you must be prepared for persecution.

I have several brothers in the prison and they began to look at me differently when I told them I found the Lord. Prison is different than out here. You have to earn the respect in a complete different manner. We call it standing on it. For example, you know someone after they come to prison and they become involved in a gang or some pagan religion for a while. Then two months later you see them get involved in a different belief or gang. Suddenly you earn the reputation as being weak because you aren't standing on anything. So after they realized that I was serious about the Lord it all came together. They respected me like never before and I was so grateful. I looked at it like this, not only did I make myself vulnerable to accept the help that was being offered to me so I could become a better person. I knew that many men behind those walls yearned for the help that they needed but they just didn't have the trust to move forward. That's when I decided to step up to the plate in a great way. I would make myself available as a vessel for the Lord to minister to these lost souls. I knew that because I was in prison, and that I was going through the same thing they were they would be more willing to listen to me than some outsider. I thank God to this day because he is the one who gave me this revelation. I do it all for him. I know, and I remember how I felt inside and I would look at these men and I could see me. It was like looking in the mirror. My spirit became determined to show them something different, that life can be worth living. I just want them to feel the same thing I feel. I feel unspeakable joy in my heart to this day.

This was the day, late that night I got on my knees in that little one man cell, I bowed my head and said Lord, tell me what you want me to do. I prayed earnestly about this friends. Wasn't to long before the Lord revealed his answer. He said Michael let my light shine through you in this dark place, I say this because you have the gift to get through to other people. At first I was overwhelmed with what the Lord said to me. However, as time went by I began to see what he was saying to me. I didn't realize that many people came to me and asked me for advice. I would question myself and try to find a reason not to believe what was happening. I kept seeking wisdom and he continued to reveal answers to me in a great way. He continued to build my faith. It was a wonderful feeling.

Now this is where it all gets crazy. The Lord put it on my heart to go to the chapel. I was like what? Are you serious? I was in the penitentiary and do you know what people would think if they saw me walk into the chapel. Man, at the time I believe that several would of fell over backwards, and some would be upset. I remember it like yesterday. My cell door popped open for the call out and I was on my way with Bible in hand. I exited the cell house, walked across the street, and went through the door. Before me stood the staircase that led three floors up to the church. I froze before them because I was confused in my heart. I thought to myself, crazy kid, you came this far you can't turn back now. Then I told myself what about all the people in front of me, what are they going to think about me, Michael Teter coming into the chapel to Praise God. Then I thought to myself, you know, everyone of them stood at this door one day just like I am now and that my friends gave me the courage I needed at the perfect time. I took a deep breath and stepped over the thresh hold. Everyone turned around and smiled at me. Now that was something I'm not use to. It was like a breath of fresh air. This is where I belong, this is my heart now live it. To this day I haven't looked back.

I was living in A-1 cell house working as a porter, and going to treatment at the same time. Everything was going well for me and then they decided to send me out to the medium facility because I met the custody requirements. I couldn't believe it, I didn't think I would ever make it out there. I began to pack all of my belongings and the fellas started coming by my house telling me to be good because it's cool out their. I had heard many stories about the medium but I wasn't interested in those stories any longer. I had a different perspective, I know that it was the Lord who sent me out their for a reason and a great purpose. Did I know what they were, of course not. I would only learn that day by day as I walked forward. At first I had conflicting feelings about the move because for some reason I thought in my heart more help was needed behind the walls. However, I am only a man and all of this is beyond my understanding. So I just continued to trust in the Lord with all of my heart because of the grace he bestowed upon me and so many others. All I can say about that is, Hallelujah!

I went to A&D and waited for the elevator door to open. It opened up and I pushed my cart into it and I was on my way. When you first get out to the medium you have to go to the clinic and get all the requirements done. As I was waiting this dude came up to the building. I looked outside and saw him and I couldn't believe my eyes. It was my bro. I never thought I would see him again. There he was with a big smile on his face. I mentioned him earlier. He is the one who walked the yard with me in Ellsworth and told me all about the Lord. I can say that he was telling me the truth I just chose not to listen to him. I went outside and shook his hand. It was awesome friends. He is a true friend. I didn't even know that he knew I was coming out their.

When you first get out their they put you in what they call Q-Dorm. You can live in their as long as you like or you can put a form-9 into the Unit Teams office to move into one of the two man rooms. He remembered that I don't like living in open dorms. He already had me setup with a room mate in L-Unit with a guy named Ron. The thing I remember most about him is that he is the craziest NASCAR fan I have ever met. He is all about Dale Jr. We got along pretty good and we learned some things from one another. He wasn't much into the word or anything but he did ask me why I always read the Bible. I just told him that is where I found true peace and freedom. Praise God! I knew that he was becoming curious because of the comments and the questions he began to ask. I would explain to the best of my ability.

I spent most of my time working out in the medium yard. I got a job on the morning trash crew that only required about thirty minutes of my day. After work I would go out and do about an hour of sprints, jogging, and abs. When I finished I would go in and take a shower because lunch was about to be served. After lunch I would do a little reading in the book until they called yard. As soon as they opened yard I would meat Brandon and Darren outside and we would lift weights for about an hour and a half. I miss those workouts, they were pretty intense. After yard I would go in, take a shower, go eat, and then lay it down until yard opened back up. I would just go outside and meet up with all of the fellas and we would just kick it unless there was a softball game. This is the time of day when people would come up to me out of the blue and start asking me questions. At the time I didn't even realize what was going on. Now I know that God was using me in a great way, I just didn't see it at the time. That's how things go in life. They will happen right before your eyes but you won't really grasp it until later. I can honestly say still to this day I have no clue what is going on. I just take it one day at a time.

At this point in time my sentence was getting shorter and I began to feel like maybe I do have a chance to make it when I get out. I decided to get involved in all the things I could to help myself become a better person and to prepare for my release. I continued to attend regular church services and my prayer life became more intense. I just started to feel the Spirit in a great way. God says tell him what you need so I dug deep down and just told him the truth. I didn't leave anything out. I just put it all in his hands and just trusted him in all ways. It's the hardest thing I have done in my life. When I did this the feeling that overcame me was like nothing I have ever experienced in my entire life. I felt good, free, full of purpose, effervescent, confident in all of my endeavors. I just ran with it and believe me I got all kinds of crazy looks but I didn't care, I knew I was doing nothing wrong. I had joy in my heart.

I was out in the weight pit one day and a friend of mine came up to me and told me that I need to go see this lady that was volunteering in the prison. I am here to tell you that my greatest weakness is women. I love women and after this long in prison I was yearning for companionship from a female. I tried to hold myself back but it didn't work. I signed up that afternoon and the next day I went to the resource center which I already planned to do just not that soon. I had a few other things to get lined out before I went there. Anyway, I walked in the classroom and there was a few other fellas in there. I seen Mrs. Ronning and there was this other girl sitting next to her. She was looking the other direction and she slowly turned her head and the first thing I noticed was her Spirit.

As the time passed I had the opportunity to talk to her for a few minutes and we just clicked. Next thing you know she was offering to help me do many different tasks like mock interviews for when I get out of prison. We learned a great deal about one another and the greatest thing I learned about her is that she loves the Lord God with all of her heart and soul. She was a volunteer from Mid-America Nazarene College in Olathe, Ks. She likes to work out, read, play volleyball, and suffers from anemia. This gave me the opportunity to pray for her. After I started learning all of these things about her my feelings were confused. I still to this day do not understand what was going on with us. I prayed that the Lord put a woman in my life that fit her description, I thought wow! However, I didn't know that he would do it while I was still incarcerated.

One day I was walking the yard with my work out partners and Ms. Bullock walked bye me and said hey Teter who's your girlfriend. I was like what. She said who's your girlfriend. I said I don't know what you are talking about, I don't have a girlfriend. She said that's not what I hear. I said I'm sorry, but I don't have one. Later that night I'm lying in my bunk and it just hit me like a ton of bricks. I had started noticing that some other inmates had been looking at me all crazy when I would be up at the resource center talking and working with Clarissa. Clarissa, if you just happen to read this book I want you to know that I apologize if I got you in any sort of trouble over this ordeal. I pray to God that you are doing well and that you have joy in your heart. I began to put two and two together. Next thing you know several different guys started asking me if her and I had something going on. I would just say that it was none of their business.

Early one morning me and a friend of mine were out in the weight pit. I was showing him the work out routine that I made for him. We were changing the bar on the rack when we spotted three black suits walking towards M Unit. That is where we lived. We looked at one another puzzled and wondered why they would be going down there. Out of no where Teter 70773 came over the loud speaker on the yard saying report back to M Unit immediately. I was like seriously. So I told Eric I would see him later and took off. When I got to the police station I opened the door and asked what I could do for them they said how many boxes do you need. I said what? For what, they said you are going to jail. I said why? They said you know we can't tell you that we are just here carrying out our orders. Once you are in segregation you will be told. They cuffed me up and grabbed all of my things and took me back behind the walls once again.

At first my mind was racing because I could not think of anything that I had done wrong warranting another trip to segregation. Then I thought to myself that it must be about Clarissa. This feeling overcame me and I just told myself if this is what it is all about then it is well worth it. I just said to myself that the Lord needs me back here again. Why? I have no clue at this moment in time but it will be revealed shortly I hope. As I passed through the wall to the other side I seen several of the fellas. They were like what's up Tet, I said not a lot, just going to jail again. They asked why and I said not sure yet. I mean you are already in a maximum penitentiary and now you are going to jail in jail. There is no feeling like it. Who would of ever thought that it is possible. Once again I am standing in front of this hundred plus year old C cell house where all the bad boys are housed for their unacceptable behavior. You have to walk up a few steps and there is this great big iron door that reminds me of mid evil times. I mean it's just like something you would see on a movie that took place during the Roman days. Huge crude iron, big bolts everywhere and a small voice that says are you serious. The door opens up and they escort you inside. Then you stand behind another door, it opens up and they put you in this small room and dress you out in seg. browns. This is a two piece suit that you just slip on. Everyone in seg is required to wear one.

After you get dressed out they escort you down the run to your new cell. Once you go inside this cell it's all over with. You are there until further notification. Once I got into the cell they told me they would bring me a bedroll as soon as possible. I believe I was more than patient, but after two days without a sheet or blanket I started getting angry. I couldn't figure out why it would take them so long to deliver one thing. I didn't act out or anything like I would of before, I remained proactive in getting this taken care of. Finally, one night out of no where a cop said hey Teter, I have a bed roll for you. To this day I thank God that it was summer time when this happened. However, the hole in Lansing stays dark. Everything is shut off from the outside and little daylight shines through. I know they allow this for the benefit of the people in the hole because when men who are locked in a small cell get to hot the attitudes, which aren't the best already, and tempers begin to flare. You can probably guess who gets the aftermath of an inmate who wants to act out. Yes, the prison guard. Out of all honesty, I feel for these guys because they are subjected to some ludicrous events everyday of their life working in the prison. They are taking a risk, most inmates hate them, I've been there. However, one day I realized that some of them are genuine and they are trying to help you become a better person. That is the truth. Some are there just to make you miserable if you get on their wrong side, that's just how the world rolls all in all, it doesn't matter if you are in prison or not.

Once you are in this little cell it is up to you to improvise, overcome, and adapt to the situation. No one is going to do it for you. You are there alone brother and that's the facts. It's all about the heart, are you willing to endure what is in store for you or are you going to succumb like so many do. Myself, I couldn't see myself giving in to all of the chaos. I took advantage of the time I had alone. I said thank you Lord for I know you are doing this for a reason, that you have a purpose for me being here right now. I spent a long time in prayer and meditation. I began to become in tune with my spiritual side like never before. I would read my Bible after I got it. I would work out for six-seven hours a day and still not feel like I did anything. I would do cross word puzzles and I would clean my cell. I had a routine that got me through every day.

A couple days passed and it was brought to my attention that I was indeed in segregation for undue familiarity with Clarissa. They hit me with a class one disciplinary report. The consequences behind this is hole time, a twenty dollar fine, and up to six months loss of good time. They hit me with all of it. I spent another three months in the hole, fined twenty dollars, given forty five days restriction, and my out date was moved back six months again. All of this and all I could say is thank you. I know it sounds crazy but by this point in time it just didn't make any sense of getting all bent out of shape like I did before. I mean for real, I did it to my self, no one twisted my arm when I was hanging out with this woman. I went back to my cell, grabbed the Bible and began to read. I did this because I have read stories in this book about men who endured way worse situations than I have ever encountered and God blessed them in the end for keeping their faith and standing strong on that rock. This gave me the comfort that my heart longed for during trials like this. This is why I know that when the Lord says you are not alone, that he is always with you he is with you. I thank God for that revelation because it has helped me so much, even to this day. I mean honestly, it's no secret, it's all right here in the good book, The Holy Bible.

So I'm talking to my neighbor one night about what we have been up to and where we have been. When our conversation was getting short I heard this voice on the other side of me say Teter is that you. I said ya, who's there. He said I can't believe it's you bro. It was a brother of mine. Michael is a good kid, he walked up to me in the chow hall one day and asked me for a Bible. Then he said you aren't laughing at me. I said why would I laugh at you for asking me for a Bible. He said I don't know, most would. I said I am not most, I am me and that is good news kid. So I got this kid a Bible and sent it to him. I just sat back and watched the Lord take off in his life. It was unreal the work that he was doing in Mike's life as compared to how he was before. I am a walking miracle friends. There is no other explanation. Now Mike is just a man as I am and even when we decide to give our lives to Christ doesn't mean that we will not make any more mistakes in our life. However, because of the blood Christ shed on the cross for all of those who believe in him gives them the ability to lift their head back up and move forward because we realize that we are born sinners and we can not move forward without his help.

I said what's up kid. He said I got in a fight out in the middle of the street. They brought me to jail. I said it happens kid, you have to do what you have to do. Then I said did you have the opportunity to walk away from it and he said no, dude attacked me so I had to protect myself. I said nothing to fret over bro, you have that right. He said I can't believe this bro, I said what. He said I prayed to God the other day that I could talk to you and here you are right next to me. He was truly in awe. He said there is no explanation to this except he answered my prayer and I said you are absolutely correct. He said are you mad at me bro, I said for what. He said I prayed to be able to talk to you and now you are sitting in the hole right next to me. I said no bro I'm not upset with you because I know it is the Lord as well. He said I don't know if I could be as cool about it as you are. I said Mike, one day you will realize that the Lord is in control of all things and it is for the good of those who believe in him. He heard your prayer and he is taking care of you right now. I said I have no problem with this because you are my friend, I care about you, and I have been wondering how you have been doing and now

I know. So I know this is God's will and it is happening for a reason beyond our understanding so let's just not worry about how we feel. This is an opportunity to enjoy one another's company. That was the end of how we felt. We just enjoyed the company of one another and kicked it.

One night I was lying on my bunk and the door just came open. I know this sounds crazy, I thought what is going on here. I mean when you are in Special Management because of your insidious behavior you just don't expect your door to pop open for any reason other than the black suits running in on you. Out of nowhere a cop named Mason jumps in front of my door and says so are you coming out or what. I know I had this puzzled look on my face, I said coming out for what. He said well, I know you are going to be down here for a while so I thought maybe you would like a porters job. I didn't know what to say. I just put my things down and went to work. It was kind of weird because even in prison you just don't get a job with out filling out the paperwork. You have to put a Form 9 into the Unit Teams office and tell them why you would be a good candidate for the job. Right there and then I knew that it was the man upstairs that blessed me with this opportunity.

I started working in the shower room. I would have to brush the walls down, spray all the chemicals on the walls to disinfect the area, pick up anything that is left on the floor. Then every now and then I would have to go in the laundry room and fold some clothes and move some boxes around. The job on the backend wasn't to bad but the job on the front end was what I truly enjoyed. After I got done in the back one of the officers would take me around each side of the cell house to pick up anything that was laying on the run. This gave me an opportunity to talk to some of the fellas that I knew that I hadn't seen for some years or so. Many of them could not believe the change that I had made in my life and they would ask me what happened and I would just tell them that I found the Good Lord. I had some really good conversations and some of them even asked me if I could get them a Bible. I couldn't get them a Bible but

I could tell them what they needed to do to get one. After I got done with all of the work I would run the stairs in the cell house for an hour or so, just up and down and around. I know at first the police thought I was loopy, but I will tell you this, it is great exercise. After the stair running I would get to take a shower all by myself and that was a privilege that you just don't get to often in segregation. I really enjoyed that because it was relaxing, not a hundred people in their trying to have a conversation at the same time. Most people just wouldn't understand unless they have been there.

At this point in time all is well. I continue to grow in my walk with Jesus Christ. I will tell you what, it has been the hardest thing I've ever done in my life. Needless to say, no one told me it was going to be easy. I still struggled many times and finally realized that it was the Lord saying draw a little closer to me Michael. During these times I would find myself just talking to him. I know some people who passed by my cell probably thought I done lost it or something. It didn't matter to me because I had joy in my heart. People could say or do what ever they wanted because no one, no substance, nothing has brought joy to my heart, nor peace the way God has. It's crazy to fathom this idea because he tells you this in the Bible as well. I am the way, the one way. That is the truth and I will stand on that until I go home. **John 8:32 NLT**-And you will know the truth, and the truth will set you free. This is good news my friends, hallelujah! I am so glad that I found the truth and it goes on to say in **John 8:36 NLT**-So if the Son sets you free, you will indeed be free.

After work one night the co told me that I was getting out of the hole. I think I was in there for only three months and many good things had transpired. They were quick to tell me that I still had forty five days of restriction to do once I got out into population. Nothing new to me, I had been doing this for many years. You can look at my disciplinary report history and see that I was a knuckle head. I had acquired thirty some report and the majority were for dangerous contraband. I look back now and I ask myself what was I thinking. However, I had to go through all of that to get where I am today. Praise God! I grabbed a couple boxes and threw the few things I had in my cell in them. They came to my cell and cuffed me up and escorted me to the door. They told me I would be going to A-2 cell house. I thought cool, I know most of the fellas up their and I have a few good friends up their as well.

I went to the police station and reported as usual. I told them where I came from, they took care of my id and informed me what cell I would be in. I thanked them and was on my way. I got down there and the co popped my door open and he allowed me twenty minutes to clean it up and get things organized. I finished that up and just kicked back on the bunk for a while why several people came by and talked with me. Just some casual conversation, how are you, where you been, the normal stuff. Before I knew it the door opened for lunch so I went to the chow hall and ate. I seen many fellas that I was hoping I would see. The crazy thing about it is that it seemed like they were as glad to see me as I was to see them. I just had to say thank you Lord.

After lunch I finally made it back to my cell to relax and read the Bible. I couldn't wait for yard. Yellow yard was in the middle of the afternoon and it was the longest yard of all yards. You could go outside lift some weights, then after you lift weights you could get some good cardio exercise as well. During the summer time it was awesome, the sun would be out, you could take your shirt off behind the walls and just absorb the rays. I would lift weights for thirty five minutes and then I would go to the far side of the track and just get sick with it doing sprints. Me and my workout partners would do interval training. I will let it be known that I have a reputation for making people throw up. I coined my workout Animal because you had to live it. It's all about transcendence, setting the bar higher, and achieving that goal only knowing that once you have accomplished it that it's not enough, in your heart you just know that you can do better. It's all about attitude, perseverance, strength, motivation, and most importantly patience. We all should know that it doesn't happen over night. It takes determination and most importantly, discipline. Hallelujah!

Usually I would work out the entire yard period, but there was those days when I would just like to stroll a couple of laps and just relax after my workout. During this time I would have the opportunity to just look around and see how everything is going around me. I'm speaking of God and how he works. I found myself always seeking understanding because I just wanted to be able to help other people. I told a friend of mine that one day and he said ya right, like anyone is going to ask someone that has spent ten plus years incarcerated for advice. Well, he's my bro and he tried to discourage me and I thank him for that to this day. Why? Because I take the negative things that people say to me and turn them into fuel of determination. It's a blessing for real, I love it when someone tells me I can't do something, it gives me what I need to show them differently. Not out of spite either, just to show them that anything is possible no matter how far you have fallen.

One afternoon I was walking the yard and this fella came up to me and asked if he could talk to me and I said sure. He said bro, I found out that my dad has passed away. I said I'm sorry to hear that kid. He said you won't believe how I found out about it. I said if you don't mind sharing I would like to hear. He said I was sitting in my cell and a friend of mine hollered out to me, would you like to read some newspapers. He told his buddy yes so he sent them to him. His friend just transferred up from Hutchinson prison so these papers were from that area. He said he was reading these papers and he got to the obituaries. See in prison when you acquire something to read you read everything because you are finding ways to make the time pass. Anyway, as he was reading the obituaries he seen his dad's name. He was just completely devastated. He couldn't believe that no one informed him of his father's death. I really didn't know what to say at this time but I am real close to this fella so I just spoke from the heart.

I said sometimes in life people do what they think is best for you given your situation. You have been in prison for almost five years now and your family may of figured that you have enough to worry about in this situation. They may know you better than you think. I'm sure it wasn't done on purpose or to smite you. All things happen the way they do for a reason son. However, I am glad that you got it off your chest, it takes courage to do that. I told him that I would pray for him if he would like. He said yes. This is crazy friends, because at this time I was feeling different. Why? Because I know the Lord put him in my path at that time for a reason. All I could think about is the seriousness of the situation, I said Lord I don't know if I can help anyone going through a trial like this. Then I realized that God knows all things before we do and he wouldn't of let this happen if he didn't know I had the ability to help Jason. I thought wow! But how, how am I to do this? Because I am only a man I still felt that I didn't do him any good. It was an overwhelming feeling that I couldn't shake. I couldn't stop thinking about it.

Yard ended so I went back to my cell house and I peeled off my restriction clothes, grabbed my shower gear and headed for the shower. I hung my things up and went to the back shower so I could contemplate the matter at hand. As I was standing under the water this overwhelming feeling overcame me. I needed to pray about it. I closed my eyes and began to pray to God about this situation. I asked him to help me understand what was going on and how am I to help this guy. Earnestly I poured my heart out right there in that shower room because deep down I wanted to be able to help Jason. I could see the pain and struggle in his eyes. I desperately needed the Lord to take this doubt away from my heart. Low and behold he did exactly that in a truly profound manner. I have never experienced anything like it in all my years.

I stepped out of the shower and was conversing with a few of the fellas, simple things like did you get a good work out. As I was drying off this feeling overcame my heart, I was experiencing something I have never felt before. I put on my boxers, threw my towel over my shoulder, grabbed my gear and began the journey back to the other side of the cell house. See, it is imperative to know that at this point in time even though God had answered all my prayers that I still experienced a little doubt in my heart. I was pretty hard on myself when I felt this way because he has already shown me time after time that he will make a way. This is the point of no return in my faith in the Triune being. Father, Spirit, Son.

As I was strolling down the run like I do everyday at this time I was touched. An overwhelming presence came upon me that I didn't understand. I know that most of you have experienced what we call goose bumps. Well, I felt something touch me on the back of the neck and these goose bumps came upon me like never before, they were the size of bee bees. I turned around real quick because I thought one of my buddies was messing with me or something of that nature. Well, there wasn't anyone there, yet I felt like someone or something was. I was in the area of cell 313. I looked over there and there was a man in the cell looking at me in a weird way. I don't know how to explain it, I never go up to a cell if I don't know the person. However, something kept telling me to go over there. The look in his eyes, never seen anything like it in all of my years, they compelled me to go over there.

I slowly approached the cell and a smile come upon his face. He didn't say a word, I looked around and seen this book lying on his bunk and out of nowhere I asked him if I could see it. He stepped back, grabbed the book and handed it to me through the bars. I opened it up and began to read, in the very first paragraph was my dad's name, Sheldon Leroy. My mind went numb, I got scared, I didn't know what to say or do. I looked up and he was just smiling so peacefully at me. I closed the book and handed it back to him. I left that man's cell speechless. I was truly in awe, I was trying to understand how this dude could have a book with my dad's name in it, and I was trying to grasp the goose bumps, and the touching on my neck. I rounded the corner and went straight to my cell, co opened the door and I went in. I got everything put away and ready for chow. Man my mind wouldn't stop racing.

I went to chow and I was completely oblivious to everyone and everything that was going on around me. Many of my friends tried to talk to me and they went as far to ask me what was wrong bro. Are you alright. I didn't even answer, at first I thought everyone was playing a sick joke on me. There was just no other explanation at the time. **Matthew 6:33 NLT-**Seek ye first the Kingdom of God and his righteousness, and all these things shall be added unto you. NLT. This is the next thing that came to my mind. I said to myself why didn't I realize this before, I guess it was the initial shock of what expired on that run that afternoon.

After chow I went back to my cell and got settled in for the night and just sat down on my bunk. I wanted nothing but understanding in this matter. I stood up, turned around and lowered myself to a kneeling position. I lowered my head to the bunk and closed my eyes. I said Lord, bring understanding to my heart, I need to know what just happened. I poured my heart out right there like never before. Then I just sat still in his presence, a small still voice said open your Bible. I thought open my Bible, so I got up and grabbed my Bible off the desk where it always sets. I opened right at **Hebrews 13:1-3 NLT** and the answer was revealed. I couldn't believe my eyes, he came through once again. It says, Continue to love each other with true Christian love. Don't forget to show hospitality to strangers, for some who have done this have entertained angels without realizing it! Don't forget about those in prison. Suffer with them as though you were there yourself. Share the sorrow of those being mistreated, as though you feel their pain in your own bodies. NLT. This is what he revealed to me, the only thing I could think of is an angel, angel, no way. I prayed again and said Lord what do I do now and he said go talk to him tomorrow at the same time.

It was a restless night, I wanted understanding about this situation in my life. I kept asking myself why are you doing this to me Lord, what have I done. At this time I didn't realize it, but it wasn't because of something I had done by any means. The next morning I got up and went to the Lord in prayer, read a few scriptures, read Our Daily

Bread, and went to chow. It was like I wasn't even there. My mind was working, I mean working full throttle. I tried to keep my mind occupied by reading and writing but it wasn't working to well so I asked the Lord to give me patience. I just laid back, closed my eyes and let myself go. I fell into a deep sleep which I truly needed. When I woke up it was time to go to yard, I slept right through lunch. The door popped open and I snatched my shoes up and went out onto the run. I slipped them on and headed for the yard to get this money. I was in need for a release badly. My workout partner and I lifted weights and did several sprints, I ran myself into the ground that afternoon but still wanted more. As we were walking a lap they called yard. I was like yes, the time has finally gotten here.

I was first in line. Soon as they opened that gate I was on my way. I took off down the street and headed straight for the stairs. I ran to my cell, stripped down to my boxers, put on my shower shoes, grabbed my gear and took off. I hit the corner with great anticipation, I got in front of cell 313 and it was empty. I thought to myself, what is going on here. I backed up on the run and said hey Mike, Mike. He came to the bars and said what's up Tet. I said what happened to old school down here below you? He said Tet did you fall off the wagon bro, I said hold up bro this is serious, what happened to him? He said bro, there hasn't been anyone in that cell for about two weeks. I said Mike don't play with me right now bro, he said seriously bro, the plumbing or something has been broken for a couple of weeks now. There hasn't been anyone in that cell, I'm telling you, talking out loud on the run like we were, several other fellas concurred with Mike. I was dumbfounded, I was more twisted now than ever. I said thanks bro and headed for the shower. While I was in the shower I asked the Lord to help me.

When I left the shower I headed down the run back to my cell. Mike asked me if I was alright and I said yes bro. I got to the lock box and the officer working the flag that day was standing right beside it opening and closing doors. I stopped dead in my tracks and said c/o, could you answer a question for me and he said what is it. I said what happened to the fella in cell 313. He said I work this flag five days a week and I'm familiar with all the inmates on this run. There hasn't been anyone in that cell for a couple of weeks because of the plumbing. I said are you sure man. He said I'm pretty sure. He opened the box up and said come here. I went around and he pointed the number out and right beside it on a yellow sticker said plumbing is broken. I was like holy crap, this is crazy. I said thank you and went to my cell.

When I got in my cell I just sat there in amazement. I was speechless and had no idea what was going on with this situation. My mind has never been so preoccupied in my life. It's the craziest thing that has ever happened to me and I couldn't figure out why it was happening to me. I did what my heart kept telling me to do, I just followed it because I wanted answers. The more I reached out to the Lord the clearer it became. One day it all came to me. What I just told you is how the Lord not only revealed himself to me, but how he took all doubt away from my heart. This is just the truth. The Bible is full of scriptures and each one of them is the truth, there is no conflict in the Word. I kept praying and praying. One day it all came to me. That was my pops who reached down and touched me on the neck which compelled me to go over to the older man's cell to see his name in that book. The fact that the guy in the cell was like no one I have ever seen before, then God revealed the scripture in the book of Hebrews about sometimes we are entertained by angels and never even know it. Why God wanted me to know it is becoming more clear each and every day. God chose me for a reason, I don't even know what it is friends.

I do know this, God took all doubt away from my heart that day and I haven't looked back since. I am only a man and I was a horrible man at that. I lived in the world for thirty five years thinking that I know it all, and thinking I know what's best for me. The truth of the matter is that I have been wrong ninety five percent of the time, which in turn led me to many dark places. Places I never really knew if I would ever come out of them. To this day I just ask the Lord what he wants me to do and he reveals the answer. All I can say about this is hallelujah!

When it all came together the way it did for me changed my life drastically. That revelation gave me the ability to live my life even in a maximum state penitentiary loving and living for the Lord. There is no place so dark in this world that the light of God can not penetrate. I am a living proof to the almighty power. I got down on my knees one day and asked the Lord to give me the courage to live life for him. He revealed another scripture out of the book of Proverbs to me. Here is what it said. When the ways of the people please the Lord, he makes even their enemies live at peace with them. **Proverbs 16:9 NLT.** When I read that scripture I just knew in my heart that it was the truth and I took heed to it. I had no doubt about it and just did it and once again he was correct. Many of my friends and acquaintances looked at me differently, like what has happened to Tet. He's acting weird these days. I could just tell by looking.

Proverbs 16:7 NLT- We can make our plans, but the Lord determines our steps was the next scripture he revealed to me. When he did that I just got into the habit of saying well Lord, what's next. I became active in the Christian call out behind the walls and learned a great deal. I got involved in every program the state offered that would help me better myself and prepare me for my release. For the last two years of my sentence, I was behind these giant walls physically, but for the first time in my life I was free. I had unspeakable joy in my heart instead of hate, conceit, arrogance, and pride. **Proverbs 11:2 NLT**- Pride leads to disgrace, but humility brings wisdom. I was done playing into the devil's hand, I had a new found strength in my heart that is much greater and truly rewarding. I laid it all down.

I began praying for people, I began sending a prayer list to the Christian Program behind the walls. I began to do many things the Lord put on my heart. Then the day came when the Lord said Michael you should start your ministry and this will be the name of it. S.P.I.R.I.T Ministries (Success, Perseverance, Inspiration, Recovery, Influence, Transformation), this is Spirit Ministries and what it is all about. I did as he asked, I was faithful and obedient to his wishes and it has been wonderful. I began to live my life for all that it is worth. I found out the hard way that love does exist and that dreams come true.

I know in my heart that Jesus Christ shed his blood on the cross that day at Calvary so I may experience eternal life if I choose to do so. Well, I chose to do so and it has been the greatest feeling I have ever experienced in my entire life. I chose to walk in the light and be led by the Holy Spirit. The more I began to understand God the more exciting my life became. Wisdom is the key and he has all of it that we could ever ask for and the great thing about it is that it is the truth. The Bible is full promises that he made to us as long as we are obedient to his word. I am only a man and I do the best that I can. I will tell you this, the rewards are much greater with God than relying on yourself for all of the answers. I know when we rely on our self we will fall, some harder than others but no one is exempt.

I have spent the rest of my time simply praying about things in my life, what I would like out of life, and for many other people. The day I got out was unreal. I didn't realize how many friends I had in the penitentiary. I took me an hour to walk from my cell house to A&D that morning. All of the fellas just wanting to say goodbye, wishing me the best, and telling me to do the greatest things. I was a good fella and I will never forget them or that I spent many years there as well. One day I hope to go back in their as a visitor to share my story with them and let them know that it doesn't matter that you spent many years in prison, that anything is possible with God. That will be an awesome day.

I went to my sisters house in Ottawa to live with her and her husband. It was quite the experience. I continued to do what I knew was best for me. I was in a new community and I knew the odds were stacked against me in every aspect of life. However, I knew in my heart that anything is possible with God. That's the attitude that I came out of prison with and that's the same attitude I have to this day and it has been truly amazing. I can not even count the blessings that have been bestowed upon me since my release.

While at my sisters I continued to workout, run, go to church until I found the right one, search for a job, find a mentor, attend my treatment group, and I joined NA because I wanted to. I know it sounds crazy, but it was the first time I have participated in any type of drug treatment because I knew it would help me stay clean. The courts were not forcing me to do it. I went on my own free will and volition. Wasn't to long after that I landed a job at Burger King. I worked there for three days and was terminated for missing work. I wasn't tripping, it was an honest mistake, just misread the schedule. I thanked him for the opportunity and I just looked at it like this. The Lord had something greater for me. I continued to do what I needed to do.

My niece asked her dad if he needed any help doing anything down on his farm and he said to let him think about it. All I can say about this fella is that he is an awesome man. Why? Most people would think that after being married to your sister for 18 years, having three little wonderful girls, and then ending up in a divorce that two brother in-laws really wouldn't have much to do with each other. Well, that is not how I roll. I have known Jim for most of my life and I never forgot all of the things he taught me, I never forgot all of the baseball games that he came to when he didn't have to, I never forgot any of the stuff he shared with me. So, one day I was at his house pulling this tractor apart for him to scrap so I could take care of my parole fees, treatment fees, etc. Next thing you know the phone rang and it was Ottawa Sanitation asking me if I still needed a job. I said yes and I began work immediately. Elizabeth, who has become my best friend drove me to work everyday from Richmond to Ottawa, and she came to pick me up every night. I have never had anyone help me like this in my life. It didn't matter what I needed to do she was there for me.

Elizabeth was the first one to tell me that I should write a book and I just dismissed the idea. I thought I can not write a book if my life depended on it. However, she didn't give up on the fact that I should do it. I finally figured out this girl believed in me for some reason. She told me that I should start writing a newsletter as well. That is the S.P.I.R.I.T Ministries newsletter that I write at the current time. I just don't know how to thank this woman. I know she is my best friend and I thank God that he placed her in my life when he did.

The following weekend me and my sister's husband fell out. I moved to my mother's and sister's house in Richmond, KS. Richmond is a small town south of Ottawa with a population of 500. I began to hall scrap metal for people, mow yards, weed eat yards, cut trees, clean up old buildings, and just help people out who needed it. I look at it as a way of giving back to the community for all the mistakes I have made. Ultimately, this is how this book came to be. God used several people in my life to tell me that I need to write a book. I finally understood what he was saying and put some serious thought into it. The only thing I couldn't figure out is why would God want me of all people to write a book. I still haven't figured it out and probably never will and I'm good with that. Some things in life are just not meant to be known and I believe this is one of them. However, I am truly grateful for this opportunity.

One day Elizabeth, her mother, and I were at Wal Mart doing a little shopping and me and Elizabeth were looking at the computers. My sister walked up and asked me what I was doing and I said well I'm going to write a book so I need to figure out a way to get a computer to write this book. She said I see, that's cool. The next day I came home from work and on the coffee table was a laptop computer, a printer, ink, and paper. I said what is all of this doing here. My sister said I thought you were writing a book, I said I see. I couldn't believe it, I prayed about it and he produced everything I needed to do the task at hand. That was May of 2010 and here it is June of 2011. To me it sounds crazy, but writing a book is like being best friends with some one, it takes time. So I only write when I feel inspired to do so. I do not try to force myself to put anything on paper, I just let it flow.

The job at Ottawa Sanitation was going pretty good. I rode on the back of the trash truck for about four months. We went all over the place. It was pretty interesting because I got to see parts of towns that I never knew existed. I got to meet many interesting people and made a few good friends along the way. It was a great workout, it almost made me tired. A truly humbling job but I thanked God for the job because I do whatever it takes to get me where I want to be.

One day I told my boss that I had to go to court in Garnett for a child support hearing a week in advance. He just looked at me all crazy and said didn't they tell you that you had to have a job when you left prison. I said of course they did but I can't miss this court date. He did not say another word about it again. The day came and I went to court just like I was suppose to do and it went well. The next day I went back to work and he wasn't very happy with me at all. We had the exact amount of help he needed that day to make the route and he never spoke to me once.

That night one of the other fellas called me on the phone and told me the boss hired two new guys and he thought maybe my job was in jeopardy. The next morning I went to work like always and when it came time to get on the trucks and go he came out of the shop and said this is your replacement and looked at my buddy and said the same thing. He took off walking for the truck while I was trying to talk to him. He wouldn't even acknowledge me, and I said is this just for today or what. He said no, this is forever. I thought to myself for a second, I said God bless you and thank you for the opportunity and walked away. At first I started to get upset and then I just knew in my heart that this was God telling me something. He was saying your work is done here and I have something greater in store for you. I held on to that with every bit of my heart and soul. Once again he was correct.

I just did what I did before. I started doing odd jobs for anyone who needed whatever done at the price they could afford and I was able to keep everything on the good side. I did a lot of work for Jim and Ronnie over the summer. It was a blessing because once again I made several good friends. I was about to go to my next child support hearing in September and still had no full time taxable job. I put applications in everywhere, even place that people told me wouldn't accept felons. I chose not to believe that because anything is possible with God so I just continued to go for it.

I went to court that morning and they weren't the happiest about my situation but they knew I had been trying. After court my phone rang and it was a guy from Fashions Inc. in Ottawa, KS. He said is this Michael Teter, I said yes. He said are you still looking for a job. I said yes. He said can you come up and see me right now and I said indeed I am. My buddy took me to see him and he hired me. I was able to call my attorney and tell him that I am employed now and that they could have the support order take directly from my check. That was a great day my friends. I have been employed their since last September and I am still working there. It has been a true blessing. They are good people to work for and truly understanding of anyone's situation. There are not to many people out there like that to be honest. As time went by they made a sign for S.P.I.R.I.T Ministries. I'm still in awe and that's what the good Lord does with those who love him.

I was led to the Community Four Square Church in Ottawa which I still attend every Sunday. I have my own website now thanks to the Lord, I write a spiritual newsletter, I have my own group on Wednesday nights, I have began to sing and speak where ever the Lord leads me. I have been blessed and it's all because of my Father in heaven and no other reason. That is why I give him all the glory for all things in my life for without him I could not do it on my own. Besides that all of my gifts were given to me by him, and the greatest gift he gave to us all is his Son Jesus Christ.

This has been a challenge for me because it's so deep and personal, I have questioned myself if I want people to know certain things about me. However, I know the Lord has a purpose for this book, I truly believe that. So this is how I look at it, if this book inspires only one and helps them all I can say is hallelujah! I don't care about anything else, I don't care what anyone thinks simply because I know what it is like to be at the very bottom and if my story can help someone start climbing back up, that is all that matters to me. Besides that, God put this book on my heart and what kind of man would I be if I didn't listen to him and be obedient to his word. Let's just see what happens. I truly believe in helping others to the fullest capacity, there is always hope.

Many people have asked me what I think is going to become of this book and I reply with this. I say it is going to be on the New York Times best sellers list, you wouldn't believe some of the responses that I get. I claim that whole heartedly with no doubt friends. I believe that with all of my heart and soul. I am truly excited about this, you never know, I may end up writing another one before it's all said and done.

I will end with this. First I thank God, and I thank God for all of you who have encouraged, stood by me, and believed in my ability to do what I do. I know I could not do it on my own by any means and that is just the truth. I want everyone to know that I give God all the glory in everything I do, I love the Lord for he first loved me. My allegiance lies with him. Lord I pray that you lift this book up because it's all for you and you alone. I thank you for your Son Jesus Christ who shed his blood on the cross for all of our sins. Thank you Lord, I love you Lord with all of my heart and soul. God bless you all.